Questioning Nineteenth-Century
Assumptions about Knowledge

I

DETERMINISM

A Symposium coordinated by
Aviv Bergman, Jean-Pierre Dupuy, and Immanuel Wallerstein

FERNAND BRAUDEL CENTER
STUDIES IN HISTORICAL SOCIAL SCIENCE

Series Editor: Richard E. Lee

The Fernand Braudel Center Studies in Historical Social Science will publish works that address theoretical and empirical questions produced by scholars in or through the Fernand Braudel Center or who share its approach and concerns. It specifically seeks to promote works that contribute to the development of the world-systems perspective engaging a holistic and relational vision of the world—the modern world-system—implicit in historical social science, which at once takes into consideration structures (long-term regularities) and change (history). With the intellectual boundaries within the sciences/ social sciences/humanities structure collapsing in the work scholars actually do, this series will offer a venue for a wide range of research that confronts the dilemmas of producing relevant accounts of historical processes in the context of the rapidly changing structures of both the social and academic world. The series will include monographs, colloquia, and collections of essays organized around specific themes.

VOLUMES IN THIS SERIES:

Questioning Nineteenth-Century Assumptions about Knowledge I: Determinism
Richard E. Lee, editor
Questioning Nineteenth-Century Assumptions about Knowledge II: Reductionism
Richard E. Lee, editor
Questioning Nineteenth-Century Assumptions about Knowledge III: Dualism
Richard E. Lee, editor

Questioning Nineteenth-Century Assumptions about Knowledge

I

DETERMINISM

Edited by Richard E. Lee

Foreword by Immanuel Wallerstein

FERNAND BRAUDEL CENTER
STUDIES IN HISTORICAL SOCIAL SCIENCE

Published by State University of New York Press, Albany

For information, contact State University of New York Press, Albany, NY
www.sunypress.edu

Production by Diane Ganeles
Marketing by Michael Campochiaro

Library of Congress Cataloging-in-Publication Data

Questioning nineteenth-century assumptions about knowledge / edited by Richard E. Lee ; foreword
    by Immanuel Wallerstein.
        v. — (The Fernand Braudel Center studies in historical social science series)
    Includes bibliographical references and index.
    Contents: v. 1. Determinism
    ISBN 978-1-4384-3391-2 (hardcover : alk. paper)
    ISBN 978-1-4384-3390-5 (pbk. : alk. paper)
    1. Knowledge, Theory of.   I. Lee, Richard E., 1945–

    BD161.Q47 2010
    121—dc22   2010004836

10 9 8 7 6 5 4 3 2 1

CONTENTS

PARTICIPANTS

KEITH BAKER—History, Stanford University, Stanford, CA

AVIV BERGMAN—Albert Einstein College of Medicine, New York, NY

DAVID BYRNE—Sociology and Social Policy, Durham University, Durham, UK

JOÃO CARAÇA—Director of Science, Gulbenkian Foundation, Lisbon, Portugal

JOHN CASTI—Institute for Monetary Economics, Technical University of Vienna, Austria; and Complexica, Inc., Santa Fe, NM

JEAN-PIERRE DUPUY—Ecole Polytechnique [GRISE], Paris, France; and Stanford University, Stanford, CA

IVAR EKELAND—Mathematics, University of British Columbia, Vancouver, Canada

ELIZABETH ERMARTH—Cultural Studies, Trent University, Peterborough, Ontario, Canada

JOHN MARTIN FISCHER—Philosophy, University of California, Riverside, Riverside, CA

STEVE FULLER—Sociology, University of Warwick, Warwick, UK

FERNANDO GIL [deceased]—Ecole des Hautes Etudes en Sciences Sociales, Paris, France

ALEXEI GRINBAUM—Centre de Recherche en Epistémologie Appliquée, Ecole Polytechnique, Paris, France

HELEN LONGINO—Philosophy and Women's Studies, University of Minnesota, Minneapolis, MN

V. BETTY SMOCOVITIS—Zoology and History, University of Florida–Gainesville, Gainesville, FL; and Philosophy and History of Science, University of Athens, Athens, Greece

BOAVENTURA DE SOUSA SANTOS—Centro de Estudos Sociais, University of Coimbra, Coimbra, Portugal; and Law School, University of Wisconsin–Madison, Madison, WI

IMMANUEL WALLERSTEIN—Sociology, Yale University, New Haven, CT

RICHARD E. LEE (Scientific Secretary)—Fernand Braudel Center, Binghamton University, Binghamton, NY

ILLUSTRATIONS

FOREWORD

This volume is one of three in a series devoted to the theme: "Questioning Nineteenth-Century Assumptions about Knowledge." The project was organized by Jean-Pierre Dupuy (a philosopher of science affiliated with the Centre de Recherche en Epistémologie Appliquée, Paris), Aviv Bergman (an evolutionary biologist who directs the Aviv Bergman Laboratory at the Albert Einstein School of Medicine, New York), and Immanuel Wallerstein (a sociologist, formerly Director of the Fernand Braudel Center at Binghamton University and currently a Senior Research Scholar at Yale University). Its Scientific Secretary was Richard E. Lee, the current Director of the Fernand Braudel Center.

The underlying premise of this series of conferences was that, in the last thirty years, scholars in all fields have been raising into question some of the fundamental premises of the modern view of knowledge, as it had been developing for at least five centuries and, in particular, as it was codified in the nineteenth century. It was at that time that a view of knowledge that was determinist, reductionist, and dualist came to predominate the intellectual scene, and found parallel expression in the natural sciences/mathematics, the social sciences, and the humanities/philosophy.

This consensus, once very widely shared, was seriously challenged in all three arenas in the last quarter of the twentieth century. The object of the series of conferences was to explore the degree of convergence of the questioning in the three arenas, which has often been clouded by the fact that different terminologies are being used in many cases.

The format we used was the following. We sought to have sixteen participants: the three organizers and the scientific secretary; three persons to prepare background papers for that meeting, coming respectively from the natural sciences/mathematics, the social sciences, and the humanities/philosophy; and nine others, three from each of the three arenas, who participated in the debate. The only persons who were present at all three meetings were the three organizers and the scientific secretary. Each meeting had four sessions of a half-day in length: one each to discuss the background paper in each of the three arenas, and a fourth in which the three organizers led an integrative discussion. We found this formula to be very productive.

We are publishing three volumes, one for each conference. Each volume contains the background paper and an edited version of the discussion (a very lively discussion, it should be said) on each of the papers, as well as the opening remarks of the organizers at the last session, followed by discussion.

We do not consider these volumes to constitute in any sense a definitive resolution of the intellectual issues. Rather, we offer them as what we believe to be a stimulating and intense debate about the underlying epistemological issues. These volumes have the special feature that they bring together scholars from the three main superdisciplines into which the world university system is currently divided. We thereby hope to contribute to overcoming the false separation of the debates caused by the use of differing terminologies in the three domains.

Perhaps in the next thirty years the world intellectual community will find a way to reunify the basic epistemology it uses and to overcome some of the limitations of nineteenth-century views about knowledge. The organizers believe that this would be very useful not only in our intellectual pursuits but in the real world to which our knowledge is supposed to apply.

We are grateful to the Gulbenkian Foundation which made these meetings possible by its financial assistance and to João Caraça, its Director of Science, who not only supported the project fully but participated in all three of the conferences.

IMMANUEL WALLERSTEIN

INTRODUCTION

The first of the three symposia on "Questioning Nineteenth-Century Assumptions about Knowledge" underwritten by the Gulbenkian Foundation was convened at Stanford University, 20–21 November 2004, to examine the contemporary debates relating to the status of "determinism" in the sciences, social sciences, and the humanities.

Participants were invited from a wide range of disciplines in order to insure the broadest variety of opinions possible. It was, however, assumed that all who took part either as authors of background papers or commentators were interested in the epistemological questions in one way or another and were ready to think about the possible limits of nineteenth-century approaches. This assumption was indeed born out by the lively, sometimes surprising, discussions of the contemporary epistemological horizon, both in terms of the problems and prospects of inherited perspectives and of possible alternatives and what they might entail not only for scholarly agendas, but for decision making in the real world.

The organization of the book mirrors the organization of the symposium. Each of the first three chapters comprises a background paper specifically authored for the occasion followed by an open discussion. Each of these first three sessions was chaired by one of the organizers. The discussions were wide-ranging, as we had hoped, and did not necessarily focus exclusively on the papers. The fourth session, chaired by the scientific secretary, began with comments by the organizers—in this case, a wrap-up by Immanuel Wallerstein and prepared remarks by Jean-Pierre Dupuy—and concluded with a final discussion on the myriad issues that had emerged over the two days of the symposium.

The first session opened with the presentation by Steve Fuller, "Freedom and Determinism in the Twenty-First Century: Prolegomena to the Rewriting of History." Fuller argues the strong position that "the sphere of rational action is composed by placing freedom and determinism in some normatively appropriate, empirically informed relationship of complementarity." In juxtaposing overdeterminist and underdeterminist perspectives as two modal logics of history, Fuller proposes we imagine a time-travel visit with Nicholas Oresme. He illustrates how different the experience might be from the point of view of a philosopher or historian and goes on to defend the proposition that "past and present overlap more than both historians and philosophers normally presume." In his discussion of Robert Fogel's counterfactual analysis, Fuller draws a parallel between the time traveller and the historical revisionist.

The conversation that followed the presentation opened with the idea of overlap between past and present, then moved on to a broad discussion that included the relationship between technology and the development of knowledge, physical causal sequence versus narrative sequence and thus the relationship between science and history, the plurality of knowledges and the plurality of pasts, representation and action, time and contingency, alternative or possible futures, and finally the determinism exercised by the disciplines of knowledge production and the material consequences of the social status of the sciences.

The second session began with the presentation by Fernando Gil, "Mobile Order: Between Chance and Necessity." Gil, the philosopher, who sadly has since passed away and thus will not be able to see this project come to fruition, takes us back to the beginning in his discussion of chance and necessity, with particular reference to Aristotle. He argues that this long-standing polarity is fundamental to our understanding of experience and closely related to the possibility of rational action, and he associates the developments in probability and statistics with Aristotle's intermediate figures: the probable, the frequent, inclination, and the spontaneous. Gil concludes his contribution with illustrations of his argument taken from the world of grand opera.

Among the themes touched on in the discussion, several stand out: randomness and determinism; complexity and chaos; emergence; statistics, laws and simulations; language; and post-structuralism as a major contemporary challenge to the basic assumptions of modern science. The rich discussion of necessity, however, was particularly noteworthy; it embraced arguments ranging from modern science and mathematics to God and religion, even considering arguments about the tenets of Calvinism. Another highlight of this discussion was the long consideration of the consequences of allowing intermediate terms to become original concepts as an alternative epistemological approach to reality.

The third session started with the presentation by Ivar Ekeland, "Determinism and Mathematical Modeling." This discussion of determinism began with a reminder of Lavoisier's basic law of chemistry, nothing gets lost and nothing gets created, and its similarity to Laplace's view that for a far-seeing demon capable of instantaneous calculation the past and future of the universe would be as an open book. After commenting on the mathematization of determinism and its application in physics and biology, Ekeland turns to economic theory and models, the Bayesian approach as a way of completing economic theory, and the lack of models of the formation of beliefs in the Bayesian approach addressed by the theory of rational expectations and game theory. Finally, Ekeland ties the question of determinism in the social sciences to the question of control.

Among the issues animating the discussion period following Ivar Ekeland's presentation the logical status and bases of the power of the field of economics figured prominently as did a debate over the stakes involved in getting rid of the concept altogether. Other questions addressed included dynamical systems and predictability; values, beliefs, and rule-based systems; the underlying nature of indeterminism and uncertainty in economic questions; and substantive versus formal rationality.

The final session of the symposium opened with remarks by Immanuel Wallerstein. He argues that historically, necessity—theological, philosophical, or scientific—has validated agency, but that now in a world that is, in Ilya Prigogine's terms, at "the end of certainties," it is time to develop a science of the plausible. Jean-Pierre Dupuy, in prepared remarks "Does Determinism Entail Necessitarianism?" compares Sartre's philosophy of freedom with its extreme opposite, Calvinism, in relation to Fernando Gil's "mobile order."

The symposium wrapped up with a series of reflections on the role and function of discussions and debates such as those that had taken place over the two days. A concern for the future, and how to approach it, was evident: Participants considered what counts as a "catastrophe" and what time scales pertain to human action; how the structures of knowledge expand our concern, for instance, to shape real human social systems that include ecosystems; and how thinking about the possible rather than the necessary, may be a more winning strategy for our times.

Finally, we would be remiss were we not to recognize and voice our appreciation for the exemplary staff support all phases of this symposium received from Donna DeVoist, along with Rebecca Dunlop and Susan R. Thornton, at the Fernand Braudel Center, and Socoro Relova, in charge of local organization at Stanford. Their cheerful, problem-solving approach contributed greatly to the success of this event.

RICHARD E. LEE

FREEDOM AND DETERMINISM IN THE TWENTY-FIRST CENTURY: PROLEGOMENA TO THE REWRITING OF HISTORY

Steve Fuller

I
THE COMPLEMENTARITY OF FREEDOM AND DETERMINISM IN THE MODERN SCIENTIFIC WORLDVIEW

There is a strong but seriously misleading tendency to suppose that determinism is opposed to freedom. On the contrary, some kind of determinism is presupposed by most accounts of freedom. My aim here is to outline the case for a still stronger position—that the sphere of rational action is composed by placing freedom and determinism in some normatively appropriate, empirically informed relationship of complementarity. The reader will see that I address the topic from many different angles without pretending to have resolved them all into a coherent perspective. Nevertheless, I believe that the considerations raised here constitute a worthy project for any discipline that calls itself a science, not least social science. Here is the guiding intuition: It doesn't make much sense to say people are free to do what they want, unless the options at their disposal are likely to result in meaningfully different outcomes that can be more or less anticipated. The only kind of determinism that is clearly opposed to freedom is the one that William James targeted in his famous 1897 essay, *The Will to Believe*. What James attacks as determinism is the belief that unactualized possibilities are illusions, which in Kantian fashion he held to undermine at once our ability to make causal inferences and assign moral responsibility. I stand with James in opposing this form of determinism. However, and perhaps more relevant to our own times, I am also launching a second-order attack on those who would deconstruct by strictly mathematical or purely literary means the freedom/determinism binary as a relic of a woebegone scientific modernism. However, the deconstructionists are right about one thing: The fates of freedom and determinism as intelligible concepts hang together not separately.

Because there is a tendency for postmodern sophisticates to associate determinism with some aspect of the modern scientific worldview, I should stress that what James originally attacked was a pervasive *pre-scientific* sensibility that the spread of the modern scientific worldview was supposed to correct. This sensibility holds that whatever happens had to happen. Such a sensibility implies nothing about the presence of overarching laws of nature, nor does the presence of overarching laws of nature imply the fatalistic attitude to the world that passes in the pre-scientific mind for determinism.[1] In contrast, two versions of the problem of "freedom and determinism" are posed by modern science. The first is associated with the *mechanical* worldview and the second with the *evolutionary* worldview. The former's intellectual center of gravity lies in the seventeenth and eighteenth centuries, the latter's in the nineteenth and twentieth centuries.[2] A good way to epitomize the difference between the two worldviews is that the mechanical worldview attempts to derive freedom from determinism, whereas the evolutionary worldview attempts the reverse. Figure 1.1 projects the hopes and fears of these two worldviews. I shall make more

	Mechanical Worldview	Evolutionary Worldview
Hope	Derive freedom from determinism (Overdeterminism)	Derive determinism from freedom (Underdeterminism)
Fear	Determinism divorced from freedom (Fatalism)	Freedom divorced from determinism (Chaos)

FIGURE 1.1 THE TWO MODERN WORLDVIEWS

of this distinction in the next section but let me start by focusing on the mechanical version of the problem, with which contemporary philosophers are more familiar. It turns on a distinction drawn by Newton's self-described "underlabourer," John Locke, between *freedom of will* and *freedom to will* (Berofsky 1973).

Locke adopted a position that has become standard among naturalistic philosophers, popularized nowadays by Daniel Dennett (1984, 2003)—that freedom to will is the only freedom worth having. Freedom to will implies possession of the means by which an effect can be reliably produced, even if the means is not a creation of its possessor. This was the hopeful message for humanity inscribed in Newton's subsumption of all movement in the universe under three laws and one overarching gravitational principle. Finally one might know what God has permitted and prohibited. On the one hand, we would not try to do things that can never be done; but on the other, we might rise to the challenge of exploiting the full range of things that can be done. This captures the sense of rational freedom in which the Enlightenment philosophers took comfort, as epitomized in the slogan, "Freedom is the recognition of necessity."

However, Kant insisted on the stronger freedom *of* will, whereby we take ourselves to be God, authors of our own fate—autonomous in the strict sense of self-legislative. His insistence on this stronger conception had two roots. One was ordinary juridical practice, whereby one's responsibility is determined by both whether an outcome would have happened even had the agent not acted and whether the agent could have acted other than s/he did. The agent's responsibility is established if the answer to the former is "no" and the latter is "yes." Freedom *to* will demands only the former condition, whereas freedom *of* will adds the latter. The second root of the stronger conception is Kant's unified view of the human mind and resolutely anthropocentric view of reality, whereby the difference between, say, Newton's Laws and the Ten Commandments is that the same modes of thought are directed in the former case externally and in the latter internally. In other words, the principles of physics and ethics are *equally* abstract constructions from the indeterminate welter of experience. Thus, in asserting freedom of will, Kant was rendering freedom to will less naturalistic and more conventional than most of his Enlightenment brethren were inclined to do: In his hands, physics became more like ethics rather than the other way round.[3]

To summarize the discussion up to this point, and to anticipate what follows, we have seen that free will presupposes two senses of determinism, the second adding weight to the first. They may be characterized as follows:

1. *Lockean determinism* = freedom *to* will = the focus is on a determined effect that could not have happened otherwise.
2. *Kantian determinism* = freedom *of* will = the focus is on an autonomous determiner who could have done otherwise.

The two positions may be usefully seen as complements: The Lockean observes from inside a system what the Kantian observes from outside it. In terms that will become salient in the next section, the Lockean is an overdeterminist, the Kantian an underdeterminist. We might say that the project of Enlightenment consists of moving people from a pre-Lockean state (i.e., the fatalism that James called determinism) to the Lockean and ultimately the Kantian states. In other words, progress is made once an apparent necessity is revealed to have been the product of contingent choice, which could have been made otherwise to significantly different effect. At this point, humans have retrieved the sense of freedom characteristic of God's point of view. It also captures the demystification of previously esoteric knowledge that characterized critical-historical theology and its secular descendant, Marxist ideology critique. As we shall see shortly, one recent philosopher who has taken seriously this sense of progress as increasing self-determination is Karl Popper.[4] But before considering Popper, we must first briefly consider Kant's unique contribution to this trajectory.

In the history of modern philosophy, Kant's status is both pivotal and peculiar. On the one hand, he was clearly a hard-headed supporter of the natural sciences on a Newtonian basis, the metaphysical presuppositions of which provided the basis for his own transcendental philosophy. Yet, on the other hand, Kant's followers spawned various schools of idealism, positivism, and pragmatism, movements that had checkered relations with the hard-core naturalism (or materialism) of Kant's Enlightenment forebears, who by the end of the nineteenth century found a descendent in Charles Darwin. In this context, words like conventionalism, constructivism, and even relativism were used to capture the sense in which Kant's freedom of will seemed to level the difference in the kind of constraint exerted between what the Greeks originally called *physis* and *nomos*—that is, the law of nature and the law of humans. This peculiar aspect of Kant's legacy became German academic dogma in the late nineteenth century, courtesy of the self-styled Neo-Kantians, in whose footsteps Jürgen Habermas was probably the last to walk. Like the Trinitarian God, the complete Habermasian human was equally present in three distinct guises—the technical, the practical, and the emancipatory—each of which constitutes a cognitive interest (Habermas 1973).[5]

At the same time, philosophers explored what might be called a naturalized Kantianism, whereby the self-legislative moral agent is operationalized in its empirical multiplicity, each functioning as a law unto itself. In a series of works culminating in *The Poverty of Historicism* (1957), Karl Popper published a famous proof of the fundamentally unlawlike—in the sense of unpredictable—nature of humans. The proof turned on the self-fulfilling and self-defeating tendencies in human behavior. Consider stage theories of progress that predict, say, a world-wide proletarian revolution. On the one hand, those who learn of the prediction may try, out of enthusiasm or coercion or both, to increase the likelihood of its realization and indeed succeed in bringing it about. Indeed, they may do so more quickly and harshly than predicted. On the other, they may try to contravene the prediction with an equal degree of single-mindedness (and perhaps perversity). And they too may succeed. This point is especially problematic for so-called real-ist theories of knowledge, according to which knowledge claims are not causally relevant—either positively or negatively—to the realization of the states of the world they represent.

This so-called proof has been taken as luminous for at least a couple of reasons. At the political level, it was read as a veiled warning to would-be central planners in an open society where information is transacted freely. One can never beat the collective intelligence of a distributed knowledge base, without resorting to stealth and deception, which is to say, morally objectionable means. At a more metaphysical level, the proof seemed to mark the difference between the limits of natural and social scientific knowledge, since planets, rocks, plants and, for the most part, animals are incapable of intentionally subverting the principles we hypothesize as governing their behavior. Whatever subversions appear to occur in the natural realm are properly seen as falsifications that result from these entities behaving as they would normally, even had we not hypothesized about them. In this respect, Popper appeared to provide a rigorous basis for the long-standing intuitions of interpretivist social scientists.[6]

But are these conclusions so clear? According to classical definitions of knowledge that clearly distinguish knowledge from less esteemed forms of belief, the sheer publicity of a knowledge claim has no bearing on its truth-value. Philosophers have traditionally given a realist spin to this point by speaking of the "fact of the matter" or "state of the world" that obtains regardless of what is believed. The point is most persuasively made when the target of the knowledge claim is not in a position to alter the fact or state that makes the claim true. But doesn't that simply reduce reality to the target's sphere of incapacity—specifically, an incapacity to generate an alternate state to the one represented in the knowledge claim? That the political and metaphysical issues can combine in curious ways is epitomized by alternative interpretations of the Baconian slogan "Knowledge is power" (or *savoir est pouvoir*, in Auguste Comte). As we learn more about the social world, what is the relationship between such knowledge and the world? If as Bacon literally said, *scientia est potentia*, what sort of potential for action does organized knowledge provide? In today's terms, is it more like a *capital* or a *consumer* technology? Let's consider these options in turn.

On the one hand, we might envisage knowledge as revealing, and hence reinforcing, a sense of order, very much along the lines of the mechanical worldview. In that respect, knowledge—and Bacon referred to *scientia*, formally organized knowledge—would consist of laws that provide the infrastructure of a rational society, i.e., the ultimate capital technology. However, an important reason these laws could function in such a capacity is that they would be *esoteric*. They would be the result of considerable and specialized research, conducted largely in seclusion, the fruits of which would be then turned over to the state for general application. A law so produced would not be subject to public scrutiny in the manner of a proposed piece of legislation, nor would there be the expectation that the knowledge informing the law would be communicated in the normal course of education.

This version of scientific politics aimed to virtualize—or, in today's usage, model—the sphere of governance as a closed system, the boundary conditions of which required innovations in the built environment that would allow the populace to be cultivated as an organic unity, a.k.a. the nation-state. Such mid-twentieth century novels as Aldous Huxley's *Brave New World* (1932) and B. F. Skinner's *Walden Two* (1948), continued to promote this project in its purest form. But even before the second half of the nineteenth century, when the relevant public works projects began to realize the project in the impure forms with which we are familiar, political economists from Francois Quesnay to Friedrich List and statisticians like Adolphe Quetelet had already defined the conceptual contours of what sociobiologists and evolutionary psychologists nowadays like to call epigenetic landscapes, namely, the sum of naturally and artificially imposed environmental constraints that foster forms of cooperative behavior, including interbreeding, that tend to render a collection of individuals more species-like, and hence with a common stake in the maintenance of all of its members, no matter how they differ in terms of properties like class, race, and creed.[7]

That Bacon—and Comte—wrote before most people (even males) received the right to vote and mass education became a standard state provision is crucial to appreciating how *scientia* was supposed to confer *potentia*. It amounted to arriving at principles than enabled legislators to deal with people precisely in the way that Newton was able to deal with natural phenomena. We might say that the research question was: How to render people governable like matter in motion? Among the relevant conditions one would have to include the erection of substantial intellectual barriers between the governors and the governed. Thus, the absence of the kind of work that is routinely performed by a stratified educational system and an increasingly specialized research culture was the main obstacle to successful statecraft in early modern Europe. Indeed, it was the very problem Plato had first identified in the *Republic*—the inability of the rulers to create sufficient distance between the knowledge possessed by themselves and the ruled. This lack of distance made figures like Machiavelli and Hobbes appear so subversive in their day: Their books purported to reveal the secrets of effective governance, not to preselected elites *but to anyone willing to listen.*[8] To be sure, Hobbes was more inclined than Machiavelli to invoke the specifically lawlike character of the knowledge he claimed to have possessed, but the overall effect of this publicity was to encourage more people to try their hand at becoming rulers, which contributed significantly—perhaps decisively—to the institutionalization of democratic regimes across the world.

This brings us to the other hand, that knowledge confers power on its possessors by destabilizing the existing social order—an interpretation much closer to Popper's own open society mentality. In that respect, it is a consumer technology. The idea that knowledge can be communicated widely, and hence used by people from very different backgrounds and interests, undermines the esotericism that underwrites the first alternative, either because the same message may be conveyed in multiple media or a medium may be designed to enable everyone to receive the same message. Popper would have encountered both ideas in the organizer of the Vienna Circle, the Marxist sociologist, Otto Neurath. The former was captured by the universal picture language, Isotype, and the latter by the more famous protocol statements and neutral observation language with which logical positivism has come to be identified. However, in either form, this alternative continues to be dogged by whether *any* sense of order is likely to self-organize once knowledge is allowed to flow so freely. Of course, this has been the hope of anarchists and libertarians but the Enlightenment's patron saints had their doubts. Here it is worth recalling how the histories of politics and science were seen as interrelated in the Enlightenment to produce the doctrines of progress that were among its signature contributions to the cultural heritage of the West.

Once Islam popularized the idea that God governs the universe by laws that bind even the sphere of divine action, some enterprising individuals now grouped together as scientific magicians, or alchemists, claimed, on the basis of esoteric knowledge, to be able to turn these laws to their advantage. Several Arab scholars and, later, the Christian scholastics condemned alchemy on grounds of empirical unreliability, as the alchemists (some of whom, like Roger Bacon, were themselves renegade scholastics) invariably overstated the field's claims to knowledge. However, the quasi-official status of the scholastic condemnations had the effect of discouraging any further testing of the alchemists' claims—or at least forced such testing underground. Just this sort of dynamic led the Enlightenment philosophers to stigmatize the medieval period as the Dark Ages from which Europe was only now (i.e., the eighteenth century) emerging, especially by challenging the Church's epistemic authority and creating alternative knowledge-based institutions, such as learned academies, that competed with theocratic university systems. However, the Enlightenment's relationship to the Middle Ages was complex. It did not challenge the scholastic critique of alchemy per se, only the course of action that the critique licensed. That was because the Enlightenment basically shared the alchemists' "freedom to will" mentality and opposed the scholastic tendency to believe that God's hands are never tied. In effect, the Enlightenment stood for a limited sense of freedom that was widely distributed, rather than an unlimited sense of freedom possessed only by one being (i.e., God).

This trade-off was at once secularized and immortalized as the narrative structure of Hegel's philosophy of history, whereby the Oriental Despot provides a concrete expression of the abstract possibility of divine omnipotence kept open by the scholastics. Though ultimately the most influential Enlightenment scheme for the evolution of humanity, Hegel's, was, of course, one of the last. What is striking about all the schemes proposed from, say, 1750 to 1850 is the way they stagger the introduction of actual people as historical subjects. In other words, they presumed a positive correspondence between epistemic advance and political inclusion. To be sure, in no country have all adults—let alone all humans—been granted, say, the right to vote at the same time. However, that brute fact is not normally given the Enlightenment's epistemic spin. Here, I suspect, we find the dead hand of Plato at work: The Enlightenment's stage theory of human development is simply a dynamic version of the static knowledge-based social structure that Plato presented in the *Republic*. In other words, the Enlightenment appreciated the order that came from an epistemic asymmetry among social classes but at the same time realized that new knowledge tended to redistribute power—in their own day, to manufacturers and merchants, who were better positioned to benefit from technological applications of Newtonian mechanics than aristocrats trained exclusively in theology and the pagan classics.

The open political question in all this is whether one could always count on the ascendant class to push forward the frontiers of knowledge so as to enfranchise a still wider sector of society by effectively redistributing its own power. Those who have said "yes" tend to be capitalists (sometimes derided as trickle-down theorists), whereas those who have said "no" tend to be socialists who believe that this trajectory becomes increasingly difficult to maintain over time without an explicit countervailing collective effort (perhaps institutionalized in the state). Regardless of whether one took a capitalist or a socialist view on the matter, the general Enlightenment perspective came to be updated during the Cold War as the linear model of science policy, whereby "basic research" generates the principles on the basis of which reliable applications can be made to improve the human condition. The model was given the name "linear" to stress the discrete sequence of basic research *then* reliable applications—as opposed to research done for the sake of application. The linear model was developed in the United States to legitimatize the National Science Foundation as an agency that allocated resources to scientists on a peer review basis (i.e., distributed by and to the basic researchers). The implicit contrast was with the mission-oriented research that was said to have characterized Nazi Germany and the Soviet Union, which supposedly tried to arrive at scientific principles that conformed to ideological imperatives.[9] The idea that monstrous applications result from the failure to master fundamental principles clearly served as a warning to those who would let their desire for "freedom of will" to overtake "freedom to will." But in the end, was the problem anything other than an updated version of the decline in social order that Plato predicted, once the Guardians and the Philosopher-Kings contaminated each other's activities?

II

FREEDOM AND DETERMINISM AS A PROBLEM OF HISTORICAL
PERSPECTIVE

The question of determinism is intimately connected with *historical perspective*, a concept best treated by taking the implied visual metaphor with deadly seriousness. I shall introduce two such perspectives, *overdeterminism* and *underdeterminism*, which are projected from the standpoint of an ideal observer who is located *inside* history (Fuller and Collier, 2004, ch. 6). In contrast, *determinism simpliciter* is represented by God, who observes from a standpoint equidistant from every moment in time, which is to say, *outside* history. This is the so-called absolute time of Newtonian mechanics, which along with absolute space formed the *divine sensorium* or, as we would now say, interface between Creator and Creation. Let me make two remarks about God here.

First, the exact location of God in such a framework was subject to heated discussion throughout the seventeenth and eighteenth centuries, as the universe came to be increasingly seen as a self-contained machine whose modus operandi was internally maintained and publicly accessible. Second, the idea of God standing equidistant from all of history remains rhetorically compelling. It helps to explain how it is possible that our best guesses about what happened in the two or three million years of hominid prehistory—or the four or five billion years of cosmological time—are taken more seriously by the *bien pensant* public and policy makers than, say, what we know much better about the very much smaller period of recorded history. When every moment in time is accorded equal weight, the sheer quantity of temporal moments, or longevity, is easily read as causal significance, such that, for example, our genetic constitution, which has remained largely unchanged for many thousands of generations, is seen as exerting a deeper control over our behavior than social institutions that have existed for a much shorter period. While such a view may be rational for God *sub specie aeternitatis*, it is not clear that it is rational for the humans whose lives occupy a well-bounded chunk of space-time. Indeed, as we become better equipped to undo several millions of years of evolution (or ourselves, the planet, etc.), the accordance of equal weight to every temporal moment may come to be seen as the last vestige of the theistic mind in the secular world.

In terms of the two worldviews introduced in the previous section, the mechanical worldview represents overdeterminism and the evolutionary worldview underdeterminism. Originally, I said that the mechanical worldview attempts to derive freedom from determinism and the evolutionary worldview derives in reverse. Now let us put the same points in negative terms: The mechanical worldview aims to prevent overdeterminism from descending into *fatalism*, while the evolutionary worldview aims to prevent underdeterminism from descending into *chaos*. An example of considerable historiographical interest makes the contrast vivid. Suppose we ask: Why did the Scientific Revolution happen in seventeenth-century Europe? The question may be interpreted in two ways, corresponding to over- and underdeterminism (Fuller 1997, ch. 5). In recent debates over the historiography of science, the two viewpoints represent, respectively, a sense of the history of science as continuous with—and, in that sense, legitimatory of—current scientific practice and a sense of the history as discontinuous with—and perhaps even delegitimatory of—those practices.[10]

The overdeterminist reads the question as implying "Why did it happen *in seventeenth-century Europe?*" This interpretation presupposes that the Scientific Revolution would have eventually happened. Thus, the interesting research questions pertain to why seventeenth-century Europe was first: What *prevented* the Scientific Revolution from happening earlier in Europe or from happening at all elsewhere, especially in places like China that had so many of the relevant preconditions already in place? Moreover, this interpretation has knock-on effects for how the subsequent history is told. For if the seventeenth-century European origin of the Scientific Revolution is a mere accident of history, then the spread of the scientific worldview from that point of origin is expected, not problematic. Again, the interesting research questions pertain to what *prevented* the scientific worldview from spreading to more areas more quickly. Given this orientation, the overdeterminist may be quick to turn to the "cognitive unity of humanity" and the various material and ideological barriers that have stood in the way of its full realization.

In contrast, the underdeterminist reads the question to mean "Why did it happen *at all?*" This interpretation presupposes that the Scientific Revolution is a unique event to be explained primarily in terms of particular features of seventeenth-century Europe that have lasted as long as they have only through great effort, typically involving the translation of the original ideas into new social forms that in turn perhaps subtly (or not so subtly) have transformed the ideas themselves. This interpretation presumes that the prior probability of a Scientific Revolution is so low—perhaps even a miracle—that part of what needs to be explained is the persistence of its legacy and the extent of its exportability: Why don't the ideas and practices of the Scientific Revolution survive merely as part of the idiosyncratic baggage of seventeenth-century European culture? The unexpected character of the world-historic significance of these ideas and practices suggests that serious odds against their success had to be overcome. Here, then, the interesting research questions concern how ideas and practices were introduced or, less neutrally, imposed on people who, left to their own devices, would have probably otherwise never adopted them.[11]

The overdeterminist adopts the standpoint of someone in the future looking backward as a legatee of the past, whereas the underdeterminist takes the position of someone in the past looking forward as a legator to the future. In terms of what may be called "the geometry of historical vision," the overdeterminist has a *hyperbolic* perspective of the past and a *linear* perspective of the future, while the underdeterminist sees the past linearly and the future hyperbolically.[12] This difference provides two radically opposed conceptions of the overall shape of history. Where the overdeterminist envisages history ultimately converging from divergent origins, the underdeterminist sees a common origin increasingly diverging over time into multiple futures. The former is due to different historical trajectories being drawn to a common endpoint, whereas the latter is due to the differentiation of trajectories from decisions taken over the course of history.[13] The opposing conceptual locations of unity and diversity in the two perspectives are worth noting here. Overdeterminism appeals to a unified end to underwrite its determinism, while underdeterminism appeals to a unified origin to underwrite its sense of freedom. The former stresses how, no matter where you start, you end up in the same place (because of a preconceived plan), while the latter stresses that even with the same starting point, you can end up in different places (because of decisions taken along the way).[14]

If the overdeterminist conceives of the historical agent as a more or less efficient vehicle for realizing history's ultimate ends, the underdeterminist positions the agent as a judge responsible for her own fate and the fate of those under her jurisdiction. In caricature, the overdeterminist treats people as replaceable because their decisions are bound to be the same and irreversible, whereas the underdeterminist treats people as irreplaceable because their decisions are bound to be different and reversible. The emotional spectrum covered by the two types of agents is correspondingly different. The overdetermined historical agent perseveres in the face of lagging fortunes yet remains impatient that the ultimate end does not come sooner—such is the inscrutability of *necessity*. In contrast, the underdetermined agent suffers regret when she appears to have taken the wrong decision, but equally experiences relief when the right decision appears to have been taken—such is the inscrutability of *contingency*.

The above contrasts are elaborated in Figure 1.2. They suggest that overdeterminism and underdeterminism subscribe to *modal logics of history* that mix freedom and determinism in opposing ways. The difference in these logics is epitomized in the following propositions:

- *Overdeterminism:* Y had to happen, but it need not have happened via X.
- *Underdeterminism:* X need not have happened, but once it did, Y had to happen.

Thus, the overdeterminist stresses the significance of the overall design of history, whereas the underdeterminist focuses on the pivotal role played by the decision-maker X in determining the outcome (at least until the next major decision is taken). The philosophy and the history of science have conventionally divided their labors

METAHISTORY Ideal Observer	OVERDETERMINED Future agent looking backward (as legatee)	UNDERDETERMINED Past agent looking forward (as legator)
Temporal horizon, as seen from the present	Hyperbolic perspective of the past, linear perspective of the future	Linear perspective of the past, hyperbolic perspective of the future
Disciplinary division of labor	Philosopher's counterfactual: they should understand us	Historian's counterfactual: we should understand them
History's natural tendency	Convergence upon one end (equifinality)	Divergence to multiple ends (plurifinality)
Constitution of history	Overarching teleology	Series of turning points
Where is "Reason in History"?	Above the consciousness of the agents (i.e., rationality can travel through multiple agents)	Below the consciousness of agents (i.e., each agent is the source of multiple rationalities)
Historical figure	Replaceable vehicle	Deciding agent
Extreme version	Vehicles too easily replaced: Fatalism ("All cultures eventually become scientific")	Decisions too easily reversed: Chaos ("It's a miracle that any culture became scientific")
Emotional spectrum	From perseverance when lagging to impatience when triumphant	From regret when wrong decision taken to relief when right decision taken
The mix of freedom and necessity in history	Y had to happen, but it need not have happened via X	X need not have happened, but once it did, Y had to happen
Prior probability that a Scientific Revolution (Y) would occur	High	Low
What needs to be explained about the Scientific Revolution	Why it did not happen everywhere (e.g., in China)	Why it happened anywhere (i.e., in Europe)

FIGURE 1.2   THE TWO MODAL LOGICS OF HISTORY

by splitting the difference between the two modal logics, with the philosophers as overdeterminists and the historians as underdeterminists. To anticipate the next section, this point can be made vivid by appealing to hypothetical time travel.

But whom should we visit? Consider Nicholas Oresme (1320–82), French Roman Catholic bishop and perhaps the most progressive mind of his century—at least as seen from an overdeterminist perspective that projects history as leading to our current scientific attitudes and beliefs. At least two centuries before Copernicus, Galileo, and Newton, he provided the major conceptual arguments against the geocentric view of the universe, for space and time having properties independent of the bodies they contain, and for the modern principle of inertial motion. Moreover, he often formulated his arguments in sophisticated mathematical terms that anticipated Descartes' development of analytic geometry. Indeed, he even deployed these arguments to debunk the authoritative field of astrology, later the bane of the modern scientific worldview. By all accounts, Oresme was taken very seriously in his day, but no Scientific Revolution occurred on his watch or even in the decades immediately following his death. The reason normally given for this puzzling state of affairs is that Oresme did not regard his own arguments as sufficiently conclusive to overturn centuries of established dogma. In fact, he regarded their inconclusiveness as an indirect sign of the unbridgeable gap between the divine and the human intellect.

Historians and philosophers see radically different things in this episode and make their plans for time travel accordingly. The historian plans to go back to the fourteenth century to learn more about Oresme's context, with an eye to rationalizing the decisions he actually took about how—and how far—to press his arguments. This strategy is familiar as sympathetic understanding or, in Popper's terms, discerning the logic of the situation. A possible consequence—perhaps unintended—of this strategy is that, upon her return, the historian concludes that Oresme wasn't really trying to be like us and so we shouldn't place unfair burdens on him. One question the historian would probably *not* have put to Oresme is why he didn't try to shift the burden of proof to the Aristotelians more aggressively, say, in the manner of Galileo. However, this question looms large for the philosopher, who would have

Oresme himself embark on a temporal voyage, with the philosopher's seminar as his destination. The inquiry would begin with a crash course in the history of physical theory since Oresme's day, with the philosopher showing how each successive stage improves on its predecessor. Oresme would duly assimilate this information as any clever pupil would, granting the logic of the philosopher's exposition. The success of such a course would demonstrate—at least to the philosopher's satisfaction—that Oresme's mind is sufficiently like ours to beg the question of why Oresme himself had not pushed this logic more forcefully. Any answer Oresme might give will appear wrong-footed, compelling the philosopher to conclude that Oresme suffered from some unfortunate barriers or blinkers that provide lingering support for the Enlightenment view that he lived in a Dark Age.

Thus, the historian and the philosopher would clearly deploy time travel to opposite effect, subjecting Oresme to quite different types of inquiry. Nevertheless, significantly, they jointly presuppose that the past is a foreign country, separated in time as if by space. The only difference is that whereas the historian treats the boundary separating the past and the present as an object of respect, the philosopher treats it as an obstacle to be overcome. But what if the past and the present are not seen as mutually exclusive? In other words, suppose we imagine that the past and the present are overlapping, with the amount of overlap subject to continual, empirically informed negotiation. This is the view I wish to defend here (Fuller 2001, 2002a). It entails removing the *entente cordiale* that currently exists between the history and the philosophy of science and, more profoundly, the reluctance to integrate over- and underdeterminism in a common methodological strategy. To explain why we should go down this route, consider the excesses to which both overdeterminism and underdeterminism are prone when left to their own devices.

On the one hand, the Popperian philosopher of science, Imre Lakatos, took overdeterminism to its logical extreme, arguing that the task of the philosophy of science is to construct an ideal history of science that consigns most of the actual history to footnotes remarking on errors, delays, and diversions. Taken on its own terms, the main problem with this policy is the frequency with which the history of science would need to be, in Lakatosian terms, rationally reconstructed as particular disciplines shift their goals and hence what previously appeared to be demonstrable errors now look like inchoate truths. This is the big grain of truth contained in Kuhn's view that after a scientific revolution, the new paradigm engages in an Orwellian rewriting of the history of its field in order to motivate novices to the paradigm.

On the other hand, extreme versions of underdeterminism may be found among historical relativists who believe that everything that could have been done is contained in what was actually done. A currently fashionable version of this position, courtesy of Foucault (1970), is that people cannot be presumed to have entertained (and hence be held accountable for) concepts for which they lacked an explicit expression.[15] A never-ending source of frustration of scientists who dip into professional history of science is that even relatively recent figures like Einstein and Heisenberg often look as if they were pursuing problems as removed from the interests of current physicists as Oresme. Now suppose historians mean to convey just this impression. How then would the past have managed to turn into the present? Is it simply a matter of "one damn thing after another" (perhaps highlighting the violence this truism conceals) or does the past contain the seeds of the future as a potential that might have been actualized earlier? I believe that the latter is the way to go, though it entails recognizing that currently the history and the philosophy of science are mutually alienated activities, which should be practised in combination, regardless of whether our official interest is the past or the present.

So what does my alternative look like? At a normative level, of course, it means that disappointment with one's performance implies that one could have done better. In terms of the time traveller's itinerary, it would require, on the one hand, that Oresme be permitted to visit us with the intent of showing how we have forgotten or distorted ideas of his that should be revived today and, on the other hand, that we return to the fourteenth century to persuade Oresme that he should take decisions favorable to our current epistemic situation. Both activities mix history and philosophy in roughly equal measures but heighten the specifically *critical* nature of the exchange, since the burden of proof in both cases is on the persuader rather than the persuaded. After all, the expectation is that Oresme would find it hard to persuade us to change our ways and we to persuade him to change his. (This is in contrast to the original scenario where time travel is designed to enable us to *accept* him and him to accept us for who both he and we actually are.) Nevertheless, whatever headway he and we would make in the two contexts would increase the degree of overlap between the past and the present. In contrast, under the current separate but equal status accorded to the history and the philosophy of science, it is hard to see how further research in both fields would help to make the past and the present mutually informative so as to serve as a guide to the future. This general field of play is depicted in Figure 1.3.

That the past and the present overlap more than both historians and philosophers normally presume may be defended on two grounds. First, there is a difference between the strictly *temporal* and the more generally *semantic* sense of possibility. To be sure, before John Duns Scotus drew the distinction in the fourteenth century as part of a defense of free will, the semantic had been normally assimilated to the temporal sense. In other words, anything possible was taken to have been

SEMANTIC DISTANCE between Past and Present	INCREASED (Minimize Temporal Overlap)	DECREASED (Maximize Temporal Overlap)
Cognitive means and ends	Learning with an eye to acceptance	Persuasion with an eye to change
Oresme's identity as he travels Past → Present	Wayward Student	Nagging Parent
Oresme's identity as we travel Past ← Present	Generous Host	Tough Customer
Implications for the History and the Philosophy of Science	They are normatively distinct disciplines	They are normatively fused disciplines

FIGURE 1.3 THE EPISTEMIC RUDIMENTS OF TIME TRAVEL

at some point actual, which in practice amounted to holding the future hostage to the past. So expressed, the pre-Scotist understanding of possibility appears very conservative: It is induction on overdrive, whereby the normative is reduced to the normal—the cardinal Popperian sin. Nevertheless, it continues to inform the relativistic refusal to judge people by standards other than those they themselves explicitly upheld. Here we might consider two different senses of the slogan associated with Plato's *Meno* that "we know more than we tell." On the one hand, Michael Polanyi interpreted it to mean that our knowledge may be expressed by other than strictly linguistic means. On the other hand, Noam Chomsky has taken it to mean that, under the right conditions, we might say more—and indeed other—than we normally do. It is the latter interpretation, reflecting the Scotist expansion of the concept of possibility that gives licence to people from different periods and cultures to criticize each other.

The second basis for supposing considerable overlap between the past and the present is that the key terms past, present, and future are token-reflexive, which means they refer equally to the user and the target of usage. When we compare our own condition with that of another time and place, not everything about that time and place is presumed to be different from our own. Presupposed is, so to speak, a common space in time that enables us to distinguish ourselves from others whom we include as actors in our own defining narratives, usually as precursors but sometimes, as suggested above, exemplars whose standards we struggle to uphold. Moreover, the token-reflexive nature of our key temporal terms makes the exact boundary between, say, the past and the present difficult to draw, as it may vary significantly across speakers and may also change in light of new historical scholarship and empirical research. At an intuitive level, I mean to capture the idea that when we refer to historical agents with concepts we use to refer to ourselves, we are treating them as virtual contemporaries, at least with respect to those matters (For an elaboration in the context of making moral judgements of historical agents, see Fuller 2002a). The deeper salience of this point will be addressed in the remainder of this chapter.

III

POSSIBLE WORLDS AS THE MICROSTRUCTURE OF FREEDOM AND DETERMINISM

Let us step back to the metalevel and ask how one needs to think about the relationship between actual and possible events in history in order to acquire the sense of perspective represented by under- and overdeterminism. Consider, once again, the case of the Scientific Revolution happening in seventeenth-century Europe. In judging the historical significance of this episode, not even the most idiographic historian means to suggest that *everything* that historically transpired in the episode was necessary for its having the significance it has had. I choose my words carefully here because I do not especially mean to deny the doctrine of internal relations associated with idealist metaphysics, according to which everything is so interdefined that to change one thing, however slightly, is to change everything else. This point can be happily conceded because it still leaves open the question *by how much* everything is changed—especially whether the amount of change substantially alters the significance of the episode. For example, a world where Isaac Newton had never existed would have certainly given us a different Scientific Revolution, but exactly how different? It might be that someone else would have come up with roughly the same synthesis around the same time as Newton, had that person lacked Newton's exotic intellectual interests or personal temperament. (The actual Newton obsessed about his originality, deeply resented slights at his genius, was swayed by flattery, and appeared to have spent most of his time trying to fathom the secrets of alchemy and the Book of Revelation.) In that case, the change would not have mattered very much to our understanding of the historical significance of the Scientific Revolution.

Historians and philosophers of science differ amongst themselves—and also with practicing scientists—about how necessary the actual person of Isaac Newton was to the Scientific Revolution. That such disagreement exists already suggests that the very idea of the Scientific Revolution as historically significant implies that we are conceptualizing it as a set of properties (e.g., mental dispositions, scientific doctrines, research techniques, etc.) that are likely to coexist under some circumstances but not others. Someone with rather literal views about Newton's genius would say that the relevant properties could only coexist in the very person Newton. But that would seem to render the generalizability of Newtonian mechanics and the spread of the Scientific Revolution a complete mystery. After all, the vast majority of those who have mastered and used Newton's equations have lacked Newton's idiosyncrasies. So, it would seem, that part of what makes an episode historically significant is that it could have occurred under somewhat different circumstances—which is to say, in some other possible world or as part of some alternate history of our world. Indeed, that Newtonian mechanics did manage to take root in many cultures and contexts rather different from seventeenth-century Europe may be taken as indirect evidence for this claim.

This suggests two general ways of thinking about the Scientific Revolution's historical significance. These two ways are based on alternative conceptions of counterfactual conditionals, or possible worlds as they are more popularly known. The 1970's witnessed a renaissance of interest in this topic, marking a general turn in analytic philosophy away from epistemology and back to metaphysics, itself a reflection of the loosening grip of logical positivism on the entire discipline. The two positions to be discussed are roughly based on the views of the two Princeton philosophers, David Lewis and Saul Kripke. (The best introduction for social scientists remains Elster [1979, ch. 6.]) Whereas Lewis envisions possible worlds as multiple parallel universes, Kripke sees them as alternate branchings of the one actual universe. This difference in overall conception implies radically different methods for constructing possible worlds, which in turn may influence our judgements about the extent of determinism in a given situation. Let us consider what is at stake in terms of the example of the Scientific Revolution.

To put you in the Lewisian frame of mind, think about the Scientific Revolution that occurred in seventeenth-century Europe as a botanist who comes across a plant, analyzes its physical composition and discovers that it includes a stable compound with some interesting nutritional or therapeutic properties that might be worth synthesizing in a different and more widely available form.[16] Those properties are like the ones that cause us to regard what took place in seventeenth-century Europe as historically significant. So the question then becomes, beyond the specific ecology that bred the particular plant, how many other ecologies and perhaps even material containers (after all, the relevant properties need not be cultivated in plants, they could be simply manufactured as drugs) could sustain the relevant set of properties as a stable compound?[17] The scientific utopias envisaged by Bacon and his successors are best seen as having been conceived in this spirit, where the stable compound they claim to have come across is the scientific method itself, which can then serve as the infrastructure for new and improved societies throughout the world.

In contrast, the Kripkean possible world theorist sees herself as intervening in a developmental process that has already been unfolding. She appears to be the classic Monday morning quarterback, the American way of conveying Hegel's idea that the Owl of Minerva takes flight at dusk.[18] The basic strategy is to identify a point in the past when, had the relevant agents decided otherwise (and there is reason to think they might have), another more desirable outcome would have resulted. At first glance, this strategy might seem to favor the overdeterminist interpretation of history, except that identification of the relevant decision-point may turn out to be quite difficult, since that moment will always depend on what we know of the actual history. So, if we want to say that China could have launched the Scientific Revolution before Europe did, what feature of its culture would have had to change and at what point in its history would that change have been feasible—such that it would not have undermined the other features of Chinese culture needed to maintain the Scientific Revolution? The nuances packed in this question are not meant to cast doubt on the existence of such decision-points. However, the answer is not straightforward and is likely to shift significantly as we learn more about both the actual character of Chinese culture and what we take to have been so significant about the actual Scientific Revolution. Indeed, whatever resistance China subsequently posed to the introduction of European scientific ideas and practices could be used as evidence that China first had to be

Westernized before it could become a scientific culture. However, this conclusion cuts both ways: By denying China's capacity to sponsor a Scientific Revolution, we would have at the same time revealed the limited reach of Western ideas without the Western vehicles to convey them.

To those who believe that history should be understood exactly as it happened—no more and no less—both the Lewisian and Kripkean approaches conjure up strong normative responses, often disguised as charges that the very idea of possible worlds is empirically ungrounded. I say disguised because Lewis and Kripke are, in the end, simply suggesting imaginative extensions of empirical practices that are integral to, respectively, the trials of the laboratory and the trials of the courtroom. However, the normative concerns remain, indeed, in a form that can be easily cast in ethical terms. On the one hand, the method of analysis and synthesis that is integral to Lewisian possible worlds is normally applied to nonhumans, or perhaps parts of humans, but not entire humans and whole human societies. Hence, the Lewisian is open to charges of exploitation and manipulation. On the other hand, the more forensic approach taken by the Kripkean possible worlds theorist is normally restricted to duly authorized judicial bodies. Here one might ask indignantly: Who gives the Kripkean the right to try people from other times and places for things they unsurprisingly failed to do because they had not attempted to do them? Having dealt earlier with the problems surrounding the Lewisian position, let me now dwell on this objection to the Kripkean position.

One research context where the Kripkean approach has been used to great effect is in the so-called New Economic History spearheaded by Robert Fogel, who won the 1993 Nobel Prize in Economics. He pioneered an exact use of counterfactual analysis to test the widespread belief that the introduction of rail transport was responsible for the massive economic growth experienced by the United States in the nineteenth century (Fogel 1964). Is it really true that had the railroads not been introduced, the United States would have not have experienced such growth? Fogel addressed the question by, so to speak, rewinding the history back to 1830, when the railroads were introduced and then playing the history forward without the railroads and evaluating the economic condition of the United States in the alternate 1890. Fogel conducted his analysis under severe historiographic constraints. He removed *only* the railroads from his analysis. In other words, everything else about the state of the world in 1830 remained the same—especially the other forms of transport and the capital available to invest in their development. Fogel chose 1830 as the date to begin the branching into the alternate history because that was the latest date the railroads could have been reasonably ignored as a potential spur to economic growth. (This is an instance of the minimal-rewrite rule, according to counterfactual methodologists, Tetlock amd Belkin [1996, 23–25.])

Note that the railroads are not presumed here to be the unique embodiment of some set of properties or ideas; rather, they are treated as merely one of several possible embodiments that might have otherwise come to the fore. Indeed, Fogel found that other forms of transport would have taken up the slack, leading to a more intensively articulated network of river and canal transport, which by 1890 would have resulted in a different distribution of population and wealth across the country, but the country as a whole would have enjoyed roughly the same level of aggregate wealth and rates of productivity. So, while the railroads were probably necessary for the growth of particular places like Chicago, they were not necessary for the overall growth of the United States. In that sense, the economic expansion of the United States in the nineteenth century was overdetermined, such that it could have occurred under several different economic regimes, including ones without rail transport.

Given how Fogel operationalized his research question, it is not surprising that the capital tied up in railroads in the actual 1830 flowed to the development of water-based transport in the alternate 1830. What *is* surprising is the projected state of the U.S. economy in the alternate 1890. Of course, the question that begs to be asked is the exact source of the overdetermination that Fogel claimed to have demonstrated. That would require identifying a point in history before 1830 when an alternate decision could have been reasonably taken, which by 1890 would have resulted in an economically diminished United States, relative to the actual 1890. That prior decision-point, though it may turn out to be several decades earlier, should be as close to 1830 as possible, on methodological grounds, so as to minimize the number of other aspects of the actual history that would also need to change. However, it is not clear whether the alternate decision would have been taken by someone in the United States itself or, say, Britain, France, or Spain, as the decision would have major consequences for bounding the United States as an economic system.[19] Nevertheless, by identifying the latest moment in history when the economic expansion of the United States was underdetermined, one would be finally in a position to address what had to be necessary for that expansion to occur.

His methodological scruples notwithstanding, Fogel's work has been subject to severe criticism, not least on normative grounds. The reception of his follow-up work, *Time on the Cross*, is instructive as an object lesson in the interdependency of causal and value judgements in the constitution of historical significance (Fogel and Engerman 1974).[20] Fogel argued, using his by now trademark counterfactual method, that slavery could have been easily sustained on strictly economic terms in the United States, had there been no overriding political will to abolish it. Surprisingly (at least to Fogel), his thesis was widely read as racist, when he very clearly had intended the exact opposite. To be sure, Fogel's argument was partly meant as a polemic against Marxists who held, very much in the spirit of classical political economy, that the agricultural basis of slavery would soon self-destruct because of its reliance on nonrenewable resources. On the contrary, Fogel claimed, the political economy of the slave-holding U.S. South adopted new agricultural technologies, engaged in land conservation, as well as treated slaves tolerably well (at least when compared to the living conditions of Blacks in the industrial North). Moreover, the South had a powerful overseas ally in Liberal Britain, which regarded a consolidated U.S. economy as a potential enemy of free trade (i.e., a serious global trading rival of the United Kingdom). Given all these factors, plus the traditional American hostility to big government imposing on all states a unitary policy relating to the private sphere, Fogel concluded that it spoke well to the efficacy of political judgement (admittedly made out of mixed motives and backed by military might) that an outcome whose occurrence had a low prior probability—the abolition of slavery—was actually brought about with long-term positive consequences.[21] More reason to rate Abraham Lincoln the greatest U.S. president, or so Fogel thought.

But Fogel's readers thought otherwise. They tarred him with the racist brush for suggesting the long-term sustainability of slavery in the United States. He seemed to imply that the default course of history—at least American history—was not necessarily on the side of the angels. He rendered underdetermined an outcome that had been previously regarded as overdetermined. That this feat should have unleashed such a moral panic reveals the extent to which we expect our causal and value judgements to move in the same direction: However long it may take, the good guys should always win in the end. The depth of our value commitments is evidenced by—or perhaps reified as—the inevitability with which we think they will be fully realized. Thus, those who have seen slavery as a moral abomination have also believed that the practice would be eventually terminated, regardless of, say, the Civil War's outcome. Conversely, those political economists who, in the footsteps of Malthus and Spencer, assimilate the persistence of poverty to the workings of natural selection have also regarded welfare programs as transient exercises in futility, regardless of the number of state-based initiatives. Very often this linking of causal and value judgements has the effect of a self-fulfilling prophecy, say, inspiring action in those who wish to see slavery end sooner rather than later or inhibiting action in those who out of pity might otherwise delay the extinction of the impoverished.

But Fogel was valorizing an entirely different kind of agent, someone who takes action against the odds yet manages to succeed. Had St. Augustine been armed with probability theory, he would have interpreted Fogel's perspective as demonstrating how free will can overcome the genetic liability known as Original Sin. I do not wish to enter here into a deep theological discussion about whether God deliberately created the world in an unfinished state to provide humans the opportunity to redeem themselves or, more heretically (but more simply), as an admission of the deity's need for humans to fill in the details of a plan that S/He can only sketch.[22] More pertinent is the metalevel point that historical revisionism of the sort practiced by Fogel, which ultimately amounts to no more than a shift in the probabilities connecting some events with some other events, can have normative consequences that outweigh, say, anything that might be accomplished by the proverbial time traveller to the past. I stress this point because the fascination with time travel associated with the popularization of Einstein's relativity theory often gives the misleading impression that the alleged changes the time traveller can make to the course of history are somehow more profound than what has regularly happened when a historian discovers new evidence and/or systematically reinterprets old evidence.[23]

In the case of both the exotic traveller in time and the historical revisionist who never leaves her study, what is loosely called changing the past involves, strictly speaking, a change in modality: A world other than our own is promoted to actuality, while ours is demoted to an alternate possibility. One's intervention in the past causes an exchange between the world that actually followed from the moment of intervention and an alternate future from that point in time. In the case of both the time traveller and the historical revisionist, the possibility so actualized need not be radically different from the world it demotes. For example, whether one imagines Fogel to be a time traveller who returns to 1830 to stop the introduction of railroads or simply an economic historian juggling counterfactuals, the alternate future turns out not to be very different on the whole—though, to be sure, different in the parts—from the one with which Americans are familiar. Nevertheless, two reasons may be offered for why time travel is typically regarded as more potent than historical revisionism. One is that people today regard the prospects of turning history in an unexpected direction so remote that the very idea comes to be associated with testing the limits of our understanding of physical reality. Another, perhaps more general, reason is that we tend to believe that the past can exert much more control over the future than the future over the past.

Even if the first reason is dismissed (though it should not be) as merely a speculative piece of sociology of knowledge, the second reason is normally seen as compelling. But is it really? It is striking that the favorite destinations of time travellers are turning points, moments in the past that we regard as significantly underdetermined with respect to the possible futures into which they open up. Had another, reasonably probable, decision been taken at the time, the outcomes of interest would have been significantly different. A good example is the moment John Wilkes Booth shot Lincoln dead at Ford's Theatre in Washington on April 14, 1865. Had Booth's aim been deflected and Lincoln not mortally wounded, the postwar reconstruction of the South might have occurred with greater perspicuity than it did under his hapless successor, Andrew Johnson, which in turn would have significantly ameliorated American race relations. However, were historians of the future to agree that prolonging Lincoln's life would have made little difference, then so too would the point of travelling back to the past to interfere with Booth's aim. Indeed, we might wish to say that, in light of subsequent historical—including counterfactual—investigation, the people at the time of Lincoln's death and for many years afterward were simply wrong to believe that Lincoln's survival would have made a difference. Similarly, we might even someday conclude, as Fogel did about the railroads, that Lincoln's leadership of the Union during the Civil War was not as decisive to the subsequent history of United States as we and his contemporaries take it to have been.

In these instances of historical revisionism, the basic facts of the case need not be other than they are: e.g., Lincoln's date of birth and death, his term of office, the duration of the Civil War, the battles of which it consisted, etc. Rather, the modal character of the key events has been altered—or more precisely, the probability distribution across the relevant set of possible worlds has changed—such that what had previously appeared necessary no longer seems so, and vice versa. In this respect, the only advantage the time traveller has over the historical revisionist is a capacity to observe the original events in more detail, which might lead to a correction in our understanding of what *actually* happened. However, the fundamental power to rewire history—the source of time travel's romance—is exactly the same as that exerted by the historical revisionist, since the time traveller's intervention is no more than a realization of a counterfactual.[24]

NOTES

1. I stress the species of determinism that James opposed because it is enjoying a revival among those who are partial to Epicurean minimal suffering approaches to ethics in an era of rapidly expanding knowledge of our genetic constitution. (Peter Singer is probably the most visible representative of this tendency but by no means the only one.) An insufficiently examined feature of our times is the schizoid normative response to the probabilistic character of genetic causation. On the one hand, the risk-seekers support the use of biotechnology for not only therapeutic but also prosthetic purposes. On the other, the risk-averse treat the technology more diagnostically to minimize the potential for suffering at both the beginning and the end of the life process. I have called the latter Karmic Darwinists and they provide a scientific version of the determinist mindset that James thought was resolutely prescientific (Fuller 2002b).

2. It would be a mistake to see the distinction between the mechanical and evolutionary worldviews as based on a disciplinary boundary between physics and biology. On the contrary, it would be more correct to say that the disciplinary boundary emerged in the nineteenth century as those who saw the universe as a machine professionally consolidated around the identity of physicists and those who saw it as a developmental process consolidated around the identity of biologists. In the case of the latter, the mechanical and evolutionary worldviews were represented by, respectively, the preformationists and the epigenesists.

3. Here it is worth remarking on the names given to the philosophical doctrines discussed here. Lockean freedom to will is associated with *libertarianism*, Kantian freedom of will with *voluntarism*. Both doctrines have high medieval roots but are rarely invoked together—and not merely because the one has migrated to Anglophone and the other to Germanophone philosophical discourse. The background metaphysics to freedom is strikingly different. Libertarianism conjures up what Jean Buridan in the fourteenth century originally called the liberty of indifference, i.e., the indeterminacy that comes from being equally drawn to alternatives because nature does not favor one over the other. Of course, as the Enlightenment realized, the logically open space could be exploited as an opportunity, but equally the best solution may lie in following the example of the classical sceptic and withdrawing from the situation altogether. In contrast, voluntarism—a doctrine developed by John Duns Scotus in the previous century—conjures up the image of opposing pulls that create conflict in the soul, compelling a decision, which then becomes life-defining. A philosophical genealogy of

existentialism would go through Augustine, Duns Scotus, Pascal, Kant, and Kierkegaard to Sartre. The cognitive psychiatrist George Ainslie has inferred from a literature survey that the will suffered a terminal decline in scientific psychology after World War I, as it came to be seen as a pseudofaculty that provided an excuse for the inevitability of war—that is, as a clash of wills (Ainslie 2001, 202).

4. In response to critics who suspect of his harboring latent Hegelian tendencies, in spite of himself, Popper concedes the point made here: ". . . that the world, in becoming conscious of itself, necessarily becomes open and incompletable" (Schilpp 1974, 1057).

5. Over his career, Habermas's relationship to Kant has changed subtly, perhaps most noticeably in Fuller (2003), where he comes to terms with the implications of the new biotechnology for human dignity. Here Habermas argues against the idea of designer babies as a violation of Kantian autonomy, as such offspring could not imagine themselves as authors of their own fate. They would always be saddled with the knowledge that they were created as a means to their parents' ends. Habermas's argument here presupposes a much stronger form of naturalism than in Habermas (1973). The younger Habermas was clear that regardless of our knowledge of how we came to be as we are, the only operative question in circumscribing our freedom in particular action contexts is whether we could have done otherwise, and whether it would have made a difference. In contrast, the older Habermas writes as if our very status as autonomous beings requires certain material pre-conditions, not least a kind of opacity between our parents' intentions and the traits we possess by virtue of their procreative activities. One wonders what he would think, were he reminded of the crude but no less real genetic sensibility that informed arranged marriages long before recent advances in biotechnology.

6. Unlike many of who have used his proof for their own purposes, Popper was himself a metaphysical indeterminist about *all* of reality, and so his point was limited to the causal efficacy of communicating knowledge claims in the human realm. He regarded the formulation of laws as universal generalizations mainly as a diagnostic tool for calibrating the difference between what we know and what there is: i.e., the method of conjectures and refutations. Popper did not see laws as potential representations of the structure of even physical reality. This is where he most sharply disagreed with the logical positivists.

7. The concept of epigenetic landscapes is due to Conrad Waddington, a key figure for understanding the interface of the social and natural sciences in the second half of the twentieth century. Just before he died in 1975, Waddington, Professor of Animal Genetics

at Edinburgh University, had penned the notoriously supportive review of E. O. Wilson's *Sociobiology: The New Synthesis* in *The New York Review of Books* that sparked worldwide controversy (Segerstrale 2000, 18–24). In the politics of U.K. science, Waddington was moderate follower of the Marxist physicist J. D. Bernal who came up with the idea of the Edinburgh Science Studies Unit, which seeded the field of science and technology studies (Fuller 2000, 327–31). Given the obvious association of epigenetic landscapes with old German racial hygiene policies, few sociologists have embraced Waddington as their own. An interesting exception is Dickens (2000, 111–12).

8. The informed reader will notice that I'm turning Leo Strauss on his head, since Machiavelli and Hobbes were his devils for the very reason I valorize them.

9. The historical basis for the valorization of the linear model as a science policy strategy is highly selective and, unsurprisingly, self-serving. The most notable example is Kuhn (1970), based on a selective reading of the history of physical sciences from the early seventeenth to the early twentieth centuries, arguing for strong paradigm boundaries as insulators of normal science from extramural concerns. In the 1970's, an ambitious group of philosophers and sociologists under Habermas's directorship of the Max Planck Institute in Starnberg built on Kuhn's observation that paradigms eventually accumulate anomalies as they reap diminishing returns on their cognitive and material investments. At that point, these self-styled finalizationists argued, it was rational to shift from basic to applied research. See Fuller (2000, ch. 5).

10. Fuller (2000, ch. 2) traces this difference in perspective to Max Planck (as overdeterminist) and Ernst Mach (as underdeterminist) in their multiply layered debate about the future of German science in the years leading up to World War I. Basically, Planck used overdeterminist arguments to justify the inherent value of completing the physics world picture, whereas Mach used underdeterminist arguments to justify shifting out of physics in the manner of the finalizationists mentioned in the previous note.

11. See Fuller (1993, ch. 2, sec. 5) for an analogous discussion of rationality as released (cf. overdeterminist) vs. imposed (cf. underdeterminist) on which the current discussion is based.

12. On linear vs. hyperbolic perspective in its original art-historical context and its metaphorical function in modern physics, see Heelan (1983), and Feyerabend (1999).

13. In the sacred historiography of Christianity, underdeterminism captures the Old Testament accounts of the Fall from Grace and descent into Babel, while overdeterminism captures the New Testament story of people of diverse backgrounds being drawn to Jesus as

pointing the way to Salvation. One might say that the secularization of Christian soteriol-ogy has undergone two stages: (1) the secularization of the New Testament story by simply altering the vehicles of salvation from, say, the Elect to Humanity to the Proletariat; (2) the secularization of the Old Testament story, which has kept the vehicles but reversed the value orientation. Thus, in the postmodern condition, Babel is valorized as cultural pluralism.

14. This difference provides the basis for contrasting views of the value of political freedom (or liberty, the Roman term preferred by the U.S. founding fathers) in the mod-ern period. The overdeterminist contributes to a perfectionist sensibility whereby freedom enables people to become *all they can be*, whereas the underdeterminist contributes to a more relativist sensibility whereby freedom enables people to be *exactly what they want to be*. When philosophers from Plato onward have tried to unify The True and The Good, they have invariably aspired to find a way to enable people *to want to be all they can be*. (When politicians attempt a similar feat, they aim to enable people *to be all they want to be*.)

15. I first puzzled over the significance of the lack of names for concepts in Fuller (1988, ch. 6), since it is much easier to see history as subject to epistemic ruptures if we require conceptual shifts to be explicitly marked by the introduction of new words.

16. When plants and animals (including humans) are subjected to this treatment—as they are increasingly by the biomedical industries—it is called bioprospecting. This activity has generated massive intellectual property disputes, especially once a Kripkean concep-tion of possible worlds is injected into a free market environment that favors a Lewisian conception.

17. This conceptualization of possible worlds is traceable to Leibniz's Christianization of Aristotle's metaphysics. Basically Leibniz considers the issue from the standpoint of the Creator who is weighing his options for generating a logically stable (or compossible) uni-verse. Leibniz conceptualized the divine mindscape, following John Duns Scotus, as trading off intension against extension. In other words, the more properties that are necessary to constitute the stable compound that interests you (intension), the easier it will be to find possible worlds incapable of sustaining that compound (extension). Popper's falsification principle turns the deity's heuristic into an all-purpose instrument for testing scientific theories, whereby, say, the universalizability of the combination of properties definitive of the Scientific Revolution is falsified once one culture fails or refuses to incorporate it.

18. Since professional football games in the United States normally occur on Sunday afternoons, Monday morning quarterback refers to someone wise with hindsight about how the game could have been played to produce a more favorable outcome.

19. In what follows, the word "someone" papers over the thorny issue of identifying the decisive agent. It is unlikely to be reducible to a decision taken by a particular individual but rather a collective decision taken by individuals distributed in a mutually recognized sphere of influence (e.g., capital investors in transport, each of whom would recognize the others as engaged in similar deliberations; or a chain of command emanating from the legislature to the administrative apparatus).

20. In Fuller (1993, ch. 4, sec. 7), I called the study of the value-cause interdependency *axioaetiotics*. I envisaged the field as experimental in the spirit of psychophysics, in which physical stimuli are varied to manipulate sensory response. Accordingly, in axioaetiotic inquiry, one would vary the causal modality of an event (i.e., the degree to which it was under- or overdetermined) to manipulate the value placed on it.

21. It is worth recalling that the dominant U.S. opinion prior to the Civil War, in opposition to the minority abolitionists, was that of popular sovereignty, i.e., each state should decide for itself whether to permit slavery. Of course, the spirit of popular sovereignty persisted after the Civil War in the form of segregation laws—at least until the Civil Rights Act of 1964. The patron saint of popular sovereignty was that libertarian slaveholder, Thomas Jefferson.

22. This view (with which I have some sympathy) is associated with St Irenaeus, the second-century bishop of Lyons, France. It enjoyed a renaissance in Victorian Britain, especially in the later writings of John Stuart Mill, under the rubric of constructive unhappiness.

23. I first explored this line of argument in a review of Barrow (Fuller 1997), which contains a section with the condescending title, "Time Travel: Is the Universe Safe for Historians?"

24. David Lewis elegantly captures this sentiment in the following comment, quoted in Dupuy:

> What we *can* do by way of "changing the future" (so to speak) is to bring it about that the future is the way it actually will be, rather than any of the other ways it would have been if we acted differently in the present. That is something like change. We make a difference. But it is not literally change, since the difference we make is between actuality and other possibilities, not between successive actualities. The literal truth is just that the future depends counterfactually on the present. It depends, partly, on what we do now (2000, 329).

REFERENCES

Ainslie, George. 2001. *Breakdown of Will*. Cambridge UK: Cambridge University Press.

Barrow, John D. 1998. *Impossibility: The Limits of Science and the Science of Limits*. Oxford: Oxford University Press.

Berofsky, Bernard. 1973. "Free Will and Determinism." Pp. 236–42 in *Dictionary of the History of Ideas*, ed. P. Wiener, vol. 2. New York: Charles Scribners & Sons.

Dennett, Daniel. 1984. *Elbow Room*. Cambridge MA: MIT Press.

———. 2003. *Freedom Evolves*. London: Penguin.

Dickens, Peter. 2000. *Social Darwinism*. Milton Keynes UK: Open University Press.

Dupuy, Jean-Pierre. 2000. "Philosophical Foundations of a New Concept of Equilibrium in the Social Sciences: Projected Equilibrium." *Philosophical Studies* 100: 323–45.

Elster, Jon. 1979. *Logic and Society: Contradictions and Possible Worlds*. Chichester UK: John & Wiley & Sons.

Feyerabend, Paul. 1999. *The Conquest of Abundance*. Chicago: University of Chicago Press.

Fogel, Robert W. 1964. *Railroads and American Economic Growth*. Baltimore: Johns Hopkins University Press.

———, and Stanley L. Engerman. 1974. *Time on the Cross*. Boston: Little Brown.

Foucault, Michael. 1970. *The Order of Things*. (Orig. 1966). New York: Random House.

Fuller, Steve. 1988. *Social Epistemology*. Bloomington: Indiana University Press.

———. 1993. *Philosophy of Science and Its Discontents*. 2nd ed. (Orig. 1989). New York: Guilford.

———. 1997. *Science*. Milton Keynes UK: Open University Press.

———. 2000. *Thomas Kuhn: A Philosophical History for Our Times*. Chicago: University of Chicago Press.

———. 2001. "Is There Philosophical Life after Kuhn?" *Philosophy of Science* 68: 565–72.

———. 2002a. "Making Up the Past: a Response to Sharrock and Leudar." *History of the Human Sciences* XV, no. 4: 115–23.

———. 2002b. "Karmic Darwinism: The Emerging Alliance between Science and Religion." *Tijdschrift voor Filosofie* (Belgium) 64: 697–722.

———. and James Collier. 2004. *Philosophy, Rhetoric and the End of Knowledge*. 2nd ed. (Orig. 1993). Mahwah NJ: Lawrence Erlbaum Associates.

Habermas, Jürgen. 1973. *Knowledge and Human Interests*. (Orig. 1968). Boston: Beacon Press.

———. 2003. *The Future of Human Nature*. Cambridge UK: Polity Press.

Heelan, Patrick A. 1983. *Space-Perception and the Philosophy of Science*. Berkeley: University of California Press.

Kuhn, Thomas S. 1970. *The Structure of Scientific Revolutions*. 2nd ed. (Orig. 1962). Chicago: University of Chicago Press.

Popper, Karl. 1957. *The Poverty of Historicism*. New York: Harper & Row.

Segerstrale, Ullica. 2000. *Defenders of the Truth: The Sociology Debate*. Oxford: Oxford University Press.

Schilpp, Paul A., ed. 1974. *The Philosophy of Karl Popper*, vol. 2. La Salle IL: Open Court Press.

Tetlock, Philip, and Aaron Belkin, eds. 1996. *Counterfactual Thought Experiments in World Politics*. Princeton: Princeton University Press.

DISCUSSION

KEITH BAKER: I wonder if you could say a little more about how you imagine this overlap between the past and present.

STEVE FULLER: We can take someone like Nicholas Oresme and make him part of the narrative that we can relate to so we can tell a story of the history of science where he is part of the history. Even if we say he holds different beliefs from us, nevertheless we can talk to him as part of the same narrative frame in which we also appear or at least our contemporary physicist would appear. It is one thing for a historian to say, "When we write about Oresme we are actually writing about this guy on a foreign planet called the fourteenth century." But for the most part when one talks about Oresme, one talks about him in relation to where we are intellectually and with regard to other topics as well, even if we do not explicitly thematize that. That is already presupposed, it seems to me. Insofar as we call him a part of the history of the European tradition, he is part of the history of physics or the history of philosophy, and even the most idiographic historians include him in that. That is where the overlap is.

DAVID BYRNE: Steve said something about "determines the path," or the "path determines." I was thinking about that in relation to the particular example, I suppose this is what you mean by determinism, but I want to be sure about this. OK, we've got Oresme in the fourteenth century. What happens? What stands between him and us? It's not continuous. There is an enormous discontinuity in European history: the Black Death. This transformation of social relations which stands between him and our era, this kind of complexity, seems very important to me. I suppose we can say there is a retrodiction possible which describes those events and picks up what you were saying before, your point about how I might get the history wrong in terms of some discrete components of detail.

STEVE FULLER: Yes, that's correct. I guess I'm quite open minded from an empirical standpoint about whether the Black Death ends up mattering. It might be true now from the standpoint of our modal understanding about the history of science that things like the Black Death do provide these major discontinuities and make it very difficult to talk about Oresme and ourselves as part of the common intellectual universe. But I can imagine that in the future, in light of evidence and reasoning and so forth, this judgment changes. The overall significance of the Black Death in terms of establishing any relationship between us and Oresme may turn out to diminish over time,

IMMANUEL WALLERSTEIN: Yes, but if I may intrude, is not the question that we should pose about Oresme a question of what his real alternatives were in the context of the time and then to make some assessment of whether he could have done X rather than Y, whether that was a realistic variable given all that we know about the world in which he lived, which may be limited? Is there some point in which he could have pushed in another direction and he could not have invented nuclear physics, but he might have done X or Y and he did not for whatever reason?

STEVE FULLER: That is the question. But then there is an issue about how does one investigate this question? And what one takes to have been the range of possibilities available to him. I think there is sometimes a tendency for historians to take what the guy actually did as the full range of what he could have done. I think that is something that I am trying to challenge, that there is a broader scope for possibility even for guys like Oresme.

IMMANUEL WALLERSTEIN: But not an unlimited scope.

STEVE FULLER: No, not unlimited. This is where empirical investigation matters. This involves a presupposition about how you conceptualize historical possibility. Sometimes it is too tied to what people have normally done or what was the average thing, and that ends up defining the scope of possibility. Whereas figures could have moved beyond that and that there was a potential for doing more that was in some way blocked. That is not easy to figure out, but I think one could push it that way and bring Oresme a little closer to us.

IMMANUEL WALLERSTEIN: Quite often almost any idea that we come up with in the twenty-first century somebody has had in the seventeenth and somebody has had in the thirteenth. You can always play the game of the history of ideas and find the nub of that idea earlier. The question I always want to pose is not about the origin of the idea but what was there in the structure of the time that kept this idea from catching on, from having any impact. It has an impact in 1983, but in 1583 the same idea put forth by some person we esteem now, nonetheless had no visible impact on the whole social scene. It just floated away or was repressed or something. Then you have to analyze the difference between the structure of the fifteenth century or the thirteenth century in Europe or anywhere else in relation to the structure of the 1970 world in which that same idea suddenly catches on enough so that it has a serious impact.

STEVE FULLER: But, you could help pose that question by addressing Oresme in a certain way, namely by saying, "Given your assumptions, why did you not actually get as far as Galileo?" Then he would stop you at some point and say, "I cannot make this move, I cannot make that move." That is a way of addressing history that is much more potentially critical of the historical subject.

JOHN CASTI: I would like to bring an example forward that is a lot more recent than the fourteenth century, but I think illustrates part of the answer to the question and it is a fairly obvious answer. This is from the field of artificial intelligence. Around 1950 when this field was being defined, even given a name, there were two competing schools of thought on how one might mimic thought processes in the human mind, in a computer machine. It is what we call now "top-down" or "bottom-up" points of view. At the time they competed on essentially equal footing for funding, intellectual ideas, and so on. The one we now call "neural network theory" fell by the wayside. This was the bottom-up view of mimicking the brain by essentially constructing artificial neurons and linking them together. It fell by the wayside due to a historical accident and a famous paper that Nitsky and Papert published that seemed to discredit the claims of the neural network people. For the better part of 50 years this whole field of research languished in obscurity. Then the publication of Douglas Hofstadter's book, *Godel, Escher, Bach,* gave new life to the idea of bottom-up thinking in AI. The scale tilted completely: now everybody is doing neural network theory, whether it is for AI or anything else. Why did that happen? It was a historical accident in the sense that this paper by Nitsky and Papert later was shown to be, not wrong, but irrelevant to the issue. The real difference, and it addresses your question, was technology. Technology was the difference. Back in the 1950's we did not have the computing technology needed to construct a meaningful size neural network. Similarly, until rather recently we did not have the computing technology to build electronic copies of some high level of fidelity of various kinds of stock markets, of road transport systems, etcetera. It is this technology the Santa Fe Institute became known for. I think that part of the answer to this question is: what is it that somebody had in one time that somebody else did not have earlier. In my view one of the most important things is that they had to work within the technology of their time, not just the ideas but what was actually available to translate these ideas into some kind of a working process. I think we could all cite many examples of this. Even, for example, the solution of Fermat's last theorem that was so well publicized a few years ago. The methods that were actually used to solve that problem were certainly not accessible to Fermat. Fermat wrote in the margin of his book that he had a solution to this problem, but if he had a solution it certainly was not the solution that Andrew Wiles and company actually put forward. The whole machinery was developed centuries after Fermat.

STEVE FULLER: Do you think Fermat would have bought a solution generated in that fashion?

JOHN CASTI: You mean if all of a sudden we called Fermat and . . .

STEVE FULLER: Yes, had him look at how the solution has been figured out.

JOHN CASTI: You know what he would have said? "It's incomprehensible."

STEVE FULLER: I think there is an open question here. You are taking for granted that it is the same problem, that he just did not have the technology to solve the problem. But the problem may be a different problem by the time you introduce the technology.

JOHN CASTI: I think it comes back to something you said at the very beginning, this distinction between the Lockean and the Kantian notions of determinism. My interpretation is that the Lockean view would say there is one true and correct rule of law or principle for answering a particular question. Whereas the Kantian view would say that there may be many rules possible and they all basically answer the question. But although they answer it and they give the same end result, they get there in dramatically different ways. I think that Fermat could have perhaps solved the problem with the methodology and techniques at his disposal at that time. There is no evidence other than his own claim that he actually did. But, he certainly would not have found Andrew Wiles's solution; he would have found it incomprehensible.

JOHN MARTIN FISHER: I want to second the point that it is very important to distinguish the idea of being able to initiate a backward flowing physical causal sequence on the one hand and on the other hand being able to do something such that if one did it the past would have been different, this counterfactual part. I think it is important not to blur those. But I also I want to try and get at the point that Keith Baker raised about temporal overlap. It is also important to distinguish between the physical causal sequence and what might be called the narrative sequence. When you talked about temporal overlap you were making a point about the narrative and not the physical causal sequence. When we talk about time travel and temporal overlap it sounds like the physical causal sequence, but really you are talking about the narrative and you are saying we are all part of the same narrative. With narrative we can go back and forth in narrative time space because what happens now can change the meaning of what happened before. So my suggestion is that your overlap idea is really a claim about narrative meaning. And even more you seem to be denying a kind of historicism; you seem to think that hypothetically we could go back in time and we would share enough concepts and meanings so that we could have fruitful conversations. And so you are denying a kind of strong historicism according to which we are not really talking the same language.

FERNANDO GIL: The idea of overlap could give real and strong content to the idea of recurrent history, which is a nice program but nobody knows exactly how it should really work. What would then be the criteria for intelligent overlapping? I think that if there is not some kind of even modern continuity, some kind of identity between the past and the present, it will be very hard to get an overlap that may exist and not simply be parallel questioning. This means that the past must understand the questions we put to it and vice versa. Your example of Oresme is a good one. Nobody knows exactly what Oresme meant but his measuring of qualities is a beautiful idea. How would we question Oresme; how would he question us with his intellectual equipment? Could he understand today's physics, today's idea of measure?

STEVE FULLER: If we go back to the fourteenth century as philosophers, not as historians, and we start with his concepts as we understand them given what he has written and what we have access to already, and we try to draw him from there to where we would like him to go, and see how far we can get before he starts saying there are some fundamental objections and he just cannot take a step this far, we will in fact be able to get different judgments about how far we can go in drawing him closer to the present. In that respect the temporal overlap gets negotiated through the empirical investigation. It is not something where a prior end point can be fixed.

V. BETTY SMOCOVITIS: I want to thank you for this paper because what you have done is recognize the problem of trying to do the philosophy of history and the philosophy of science. I'm not sure that we have a solution but perhaps we have a way of reconceiving it, reproblematizing it to get us out of a series of traps. I still think you believe it is possible to have a coherent narrative. I want to ask you, is there such a thing as coherent narrative?

STEVE FULLER: I'm not saying ultimate, I mean small *c* small *n* here. And one that is empirically corrigible over time. I'm not putting forward some kind of absolutist conception.

V. BETTY SMOCOVITIS: But that is the problem it seems to me. The problem is, as John [Martin Fisher] said, the narrativity of history and also the narrativity of science. I work in evolutionary science so I see narrative patterns in evolutionary science. As someone who has at least tried to delve into a little bit of philosophy of history, it seems to me that narrativity is where one finds past, present, and future. There is a determinism that can emerge from particular kinds of narratives that are unproblematized. That is what we mean by unifying narratives, for example. I think we ought to talk about narratives, the kinds of problems that historians have; that is the other worry I have. I don't think figuring out what Oresme thought, or the kinds of technology of an epoch, or what kind of an event was the scientific revolution, is really meaningful to many of us in history because what we do now is problematize the event as an event. What makes it count as an event? I think we need to be careful about the scientific revolution and what it is.

I think we may want to discuss the *Guns, Germs, and Steel* problem. Do you all know the book by Jared Diamond? It is a troubling narrative, a troubling history of the world that begins with a question that he thinks is entirely benign, devoid of any kind of a political or generational context. Why is it that the Papuans in Papua/New Guinea don't get cargo, don't get all this stuff? He proceeds to answer why they do not have the fruits of science and technology chapter by chapter, taking us through the history of the discipline, all the way through the history of knowledge, and emerges with the answer. Well, it is really that you can't blame them. I have been in reading groups with colleagues who came out of the 1960's, liberal American elites who view this as politically liberating. I view it as patronizing, condescending historiography that makes elite American intellectuals feel good about what they do. Papuans could not possibly have gotten this stuff but they are just as legitimate and valid in their forms of knowledge and their culture.

HELEN LONGINO: I want to go back to the overlap question because it seems to me that in talking about identifying overlaps, we were trying to think if we could speak the same language as Oresme. That seems to be only part of the overlap issue about the relation between past, present, and future, because there can be overlaps that are identified in other ways than through the mutual understanding of protagonists in the past and protagonists in the present and our imagined protagonists in the future. There can be overlap through continuities of processes that have nothing to do with, that are independent of, how we are thinking about them, and of how our ancestors might have thought about them. I am not sure that we are getting very far when we try to debate about whether or not we can cross that conceptual gulf between ourselves and the fourteenth century. And the other thing, when you were talking, John [Martin Fisher], and you wanted to bring us back to Steve [Fuller]'s earlier Lockean-Kantian distinction I thought you were going to take it in a slightly different way. As I understand the Lockean distinction, it is not so much freedom of will but freedom to act, that is, freedom to act on our desires, which is more the way Hume conceived it, that is not being hindered by external obstacles such as the lack of computational methodology that would enable us to solve or prove Fermat's theorem, or work with the neural network model, for example; all this we can do now, but we could not do before. So there is that issue of the availability of technology. There is a separate issue when we are thinking about ourselves and Oresme, or at least the way the Oresme issue was framed, and that is why did not Oresme think about this differently? There are two different kinds of reasons. It might be whatever was going on for him, but there is also what was available for him to think with. I think those are two quite different ways of thinking that we have to keep in mind if we are going to engage in this thought experiment of time travel. What is it that we are traveling through, in fact to?

JEAN-PIERRE DUPUY: In French we do not spontaneously make the difference between a made-up story and History, with a capital *H*. There is a good example: a Hollywood screenplay. I've been told that screenwriters test the endings before audiences. How do you do that? You have the story, it is a made-up story, events take place but they must obey causal laws. If we change the ending we are going to change the meaning of all the events that take place, all the possible events. There are more and more movies whose ending comes as a radical surprise and changes completely what we thought was the meaning of the root story. *Seven* is a case in point. Yes, *Vertigo* too! So if the made-up story is well designed then the loop must loop back onto itself. That is, events of the story must causally produce within the story, the ending. But we're not talking here about made-up stories. We are talking about history and this point is absolutely fundamental. Sartre pushed Kant's concept of liberty to the limit. For Sartre we can choose everything including the past and include the fact that we were born, because we can always commit suicide if we are not happy with our lives. In Sartre's *Being and Nothingness* there is this notion that the future bestows meaning on the past. But as long as history continues, for example, history has no ending, then the meaning of the past is always suspended.

IMMANUEL WALLERSTEIN: That's the famous Mao Zedong joke: what do you think of the French Revolution? It's too early to tell!

BOAVENTURA DE SOUSA SANTOS: I'm trying to think of a kind of social science perspective on this discussion. By asking and discussing these issues are we being prevented from asking other questions that may be probably more relevant from my point of view. It really comes round to what matters. The quest for transparency does not address a crucial issue for me, which is the impossibility of knowledge. The second issue is the question of the plurality of knowledge. You assume in this discussion there is a single form of knowledge and this is for me quite objectionable. I think there is a plurality of knowledges and if you consider that, then probably there is a plurality of pasts. As a sociologist I am very concerned with that. Because of the Western bias of the unity of knowledge, we have assumed that the plurality of pasts could turn into a single present, the idea of modernization, of development, so on, but then that is different pasts in a single present. So I propose to you an alternative view of this. What I am concerned about is alternative futures. Suppose that you have kinds of knowledges and constructions that would allow us to see alternative pasts and then the present. The present is the way in which we make sense of this plurality; therefore, it is a transient type of moment and the present is nothing but this, all these different pasts are in fact now consumed in a single form. It's a *bricolage*. The present is a *bricolage* of this palimpsest. This is a palimpsest for all of us and we have some indigenous pasts in our lives. Therefore from here we can think of our alternative futures.

ALEXEI GRINBAUM: There is no fixed past at which you look. You are here and you learn something about what happened at t_1. So the 1 is here. Here is information. And then you say: Oh, at t_1 there was such and such an event. But then of course when you were at t_1, you were not in position to say that there was an event. You didn't know anything about that. So it happens that at t_2 you constitute the history, you constitute an event that had happened previously at t_1.

IMMANUEL WALLERSTEIN: If I can intrude the old Yugoslav or Balkan cynicism, the only thing sure is the future because the past always changes. I think that's something structurally we have to bear in mind.

DAVID BYRNE: It strikes me that we've got a problem of representation which is one thing and a problem of action which is another. Now I am very much an applied social scientist so I'm trying to work with people who are constantly saying what will happen if we do this? What will be the consequences either at the microlevel or even at the middle-range level? And one of the things which is quite interesting for me is the technologies that are available. And with this idea of configuration, I kept thinking about Steve's paper, what would Norbert Elias say about all this? You know the idea of configurational causation, different patterns of things that come together to produce events. And that I think is the point that was raised about action. That is, in the sociologist's conception of the world there are the human actors that in one way or another have the possibility of creating different kinds of outcomes. The reflection on what has happened, which may be very different from the traditional kinds of determinism because configuration implies different sets of things can produce the same result, is one of the technologies we bring to bear on informed social actions. I am interested partially in the ideas about representation or the story in the past, but I am interested primarily because that is information that leads into decision-making processes. Neural net technology is a very good example. Neural net technology is booming now partly because there is a technological base for it but also because there is a commercial and policy-makers' use for it. We are right in the middle of an area where people make billions of dollars out of neural net technology. But usages include trivial decisions about consumer preferences in supermarkets.

JOHN MARTIN FISHER: On the distinction between the Lockean and the Kantian approaches I would put it somewhat differently. It in a way goes back to the dilemma William James presented in *The Dilemma of Determinism*, that is, a very intuitive dilemma according to James: either causal determinism is true or it is false. If it is true then we could not have done otherwise, and we had to do what we did and so we are not responsible. But if determinism was false, well then everything is random and accidental and it is not me, I am not making the difference. The difference happens but I am not making it. So I think the Kantian point you make is that we feel we want alternative possibilities. We want it to be the case that we could have done otherwise, that we did not have to do what we did. But the Lockean point is that my choice has to flow from me. It cannot be something accidental or random. I try to link the two by saying one way of thinking about what matters is that I make the difference to the world through my free choices. Part of what is important is making the difference and part of it is that it has to be flowing from me, it cannot just be luck. So I think there are similar points there. I would also like to note that I do not think we should dismiss quickly the ideal that you could accept indeterminism and still have some kind of predictability and rational expectations. There are a number of philosophers now who write about action who seek to give an indeterministic account of agency consistent with moral responsibility and rationality. So they give an account of acting for reasons that are not deterministic.

JOÃO CARAÇA: I think this discussion has been very interesting and very focused on the social sciences which was in fact to the point because this question of past, present, and future is really central to the social sciences, but not to other fields of knowledge maybe, but we are considering it now.

IMMANUEL WALLERSTEIN: Maybe it should be central to the other fields of knowledge.

JOÃO CARAÇA: No, it is there, like in science it is there, but it is not the object of the exercise: maybe to predict something but it is with the object of using it.

I would like to bring in a Portuguese poet. He says that even the past is forever uncertain. Now we are talking about overlap, and John Casti talked about technology. So some things are equal or so they seem. They are continuous. And some things then just change, like technology. So people's understanding, people's relationship with nature, with reality, changes. It is those changes in fact, that bring about the incompatibility of understanding. It is a succession of presents and because we live in the presents, we tend to say they are clear because we flow through them. But we are not sure. It depends very much upon what people focus their minds. This question of past, present, and future from a physicist's point of view is really showing that the social sciences are still in the classical period, like classical mechanics, where time is a parameter, where time is something that is outside and it flows from negative infinity to positive infinity. They have not yet made the change that physics has, especially the question that quantum mechanics has thought about—incompatibility. The central theme of quantum mechanics is in fact that some things, some parameters are incompatible with others. For instance, we now know that we cannot measure position and speed of an electron or particles; they are incompatible. Now the question of narrative is very interesting because narrative is closed. We look at the book and narrative is there. We look at a film, and film is there. If the ending is somehow out of sense, it makes us reconsider the narrative, but it is there. And the best example for that is the CDROM or DVD. We have a DVD and everything is in there. There is no time; you have all the frames there and they have been read in one sense and it makes a story. If it is read the other way around, it has no sense. So in fact, in the DVD then, time is not there. This question of narrative in social science shows, because we understand the world now with complexity, the need for openness.

AVIV BERGMAN: Maybe we are dealing with an unquestion. Maybe there is a physics envy here to something that physicists no longer believe in, no longer take into account, or do not care about. My main concern with this debate is whether we can really talk about determinism in the sciences, where science's concerns don't really pay any attention to this issue at all. And I would also like to bring the conversation to the issue of what comes from the dynamical system point of view: it is much harder to predict the past than to predict the future. This brings the issue of how can we choose among all the possible pasts the one that is most probable or most probabilistically explanatory.

IMMANUEL WALLERSTEIN: Perhaps the question is which past is most useful?

ELIZABETH (BETSY) ERMARTH: We are taking for granted the common denominator universe in everything we say. We talk about past, present, and future. I don't care whether it's possible futures or possible pasts, we're still talking about a common denominator universe and that common denominator of them all, among others, is time—a certain idea of time as a neutral medium in which mutually-informative measurements can be made. It has been with us for a very long time, ever since Einstein, who developed his thinking when he realized that time was suspect, as he said. It seems to me that that common denominator is what we need to challenge. That really leads to a pretty unnerving either/or question, or is this an either/or question? Do we look for common denominators, which by definition are universal at least within a pretty wide parameter? Or do we hold our noses and jump into transience, the constitutive practice and process which is ever ongoing and never finished and in which order is a phase, and the structures and the possibilities of that order end completely, and possibly if Nabokov is right, every three seconds. You are constantly reinventing your mental structure, you blink and your consciousness is reborn, that is a little exaggerated, but it is a kind of metaphor for the artistic effort that we are all engaged in and all the time fooling ourselves by our retreating into a kind of identity and discussion in common language that falls apart as we speak it. Is it an either/or?

ALEXEI GRINBAUM: Time arises in the process of neglect of information. What does that mean? It means that if you wanted to produce intersubjective discourse you have to neglect something in the individual sets of information.

ELIZABETH (BETSY) ERMARTH: Does that time come to an end, then?

AVIV BERGMAN: In other words does the choice of what you neglect change the meaning?

ALEXEI GRINBAUM: There are endless ends of time, every time you get new information you update and the previous thing gets updated. But now of course you want to do it so that the inflow of new information does not change this big intersubjective notion of time. On the one hand you endlessly update so you endlessly change your own concept of time. But then the neglect works so that there is no end of time. Well, I am not speaking about general relativity. You neglect enough information so that there is discontinuity. There is this notion of complementarity. Philosophy has to learn this lesson from quantum physics, get it to other fields like psychology or some other social sciences. Those fields can use this philosophy of complementarity perhaps by giving a different sense to the word complementarity. But there are always things which then get together at the same time which cannot be observed together, etc. It works very well in a very small number of disciplines. It works basically only for something like phenomenology or psychology based on phenomenology. The problem is about language because the exact sciences, unlike the social sciences, cannot all speak ordinary language, they speak a special, formalized language. And the social sciences have an ambition to speak a language as close to the ordinary as possible because they speak to decision makers, sociologists speak to the public, etc. There is a constitution of history because the language of the discipline requires that there be a linear past future line. So I'm very pessimistic about the prospects of going and teaching social sciences any lessons from the sciences with specialized languages.

JOHN CASTI: I'm a little uncomfortable with a temporal picture looking through a fixed point. From the dynamical systems perspective, I don't see any a priori reason to believe there is any fixed point. There will be an attractor of some kind but a fixed point is pretty unlikely in my view. What I would like to suggest is a different science fiction picture, but one that focuses not on time but on space.

Suppose that—and you could either think about it here on this planet, but I like to think about it in extraterrestrial terms—we go off into the other side of the galaxy and there is a second Earth out there where physically and in virtually every other way it is identical to this one and it is populated by people who have every semblance of looking like us and we go to them and ask how do they actually see this world? It is really a question: could we possibly understand them? Or is it just a historical lack? We as physicists for example, describe the world in terms of certain conceptual categories that are actually rather arbitrary: location, velocity, energy, etc. These are choices that were made a long time ago and have percolated down through the centuries into what we think of as something approximating a coherent picture of how to describe the world around us. But I wonder if we were off on that second Earth, and this pertains even to the question that people often pose about communication with extraterrestrial intelligence, could we have any kind of meaningful communication even at such a basic level as the physical environment? In mathematical terms, one might say, would their conceptual way of framing what the issues are in their world be isomorphic to the one that we use on this planet? I'm a little bit skeptical about it. And we have examples of rather grand failures at attempts to communicate with other intelligent beings on this planet, dolphins, chimpanzees, and whatever, other humans.

ALEXEI GRINBAUM: Technical point: do you imagine that natural things are the same or the technological artificial world is also the same?

JOHN CASTI: Well let's just say the physical natural world for the sake of discussion.

IMMANUEL WALLERSTEIN: So what is different is the social world. Because the physical world is identical but the perception of the universe is different.

JOHN CASTI: But the way that you conceptualize that may or may not be different. That is the question. Is it isomorphic? It will probably look different superficially. Then maybe they will not use numbers, maybe they will use lengths or something to conceptualize the distances. But even here on this planet, we are not able to enter into any kind of meaningful communication with organisms with which we share a very long evolutionary history. Try and talk to an octopus. They show lots of signs of intelligence. So do chimpanzees for that matter, but all attempts that were made to have meaningful interaction or communications have been, in my opinion, dismal failures. They are great experiments to read about but in the end we do not learn anything about what it's like to be an octopus because they seemingly conceptualize the very same physical environment in a radically different way. Or maybe they don't. Maybe they have a secret to the universe, they just can't speak. It is hard to say. The point is that this temporal picture which Betsy [Elizabeth Ermarth] pointed out has a lot of question marks attached to it. I think one can equally well think about a spatial example that has at least as many question marks, they are just different ones.

KEITH BAKER: The absolute end of determinacy, determinism, is the absence of time. It is simultaneity. So basically time is the way in which we deal with uncertainty. In every domain we deal with uncertainty because time is the only way it seems that we can deal with that. If that is true then that says something about narrative. I do not think narratives are closed. Narratives are open. What we're talking about here is set of narratives which offer openings to the future. So there are very few utterly closed narratives. Even the most closed narrative, what would it say? It would say, do nothing in the future. It would have an implication for the future. So narratives always open up some possibilities and it seems to me that the same is true of representation and action. One cannot make a clear distinction between representation and action. To represent something is already doing something. To represent is to act. It is performative. If you represent something then you are in fact not only doing something, you are making arguments for doing further things. What we can agree on, maybe, is that there are different possible pasts, that is to say different narratives that lead to different definitions of the situation in the present, and also open up into various kinds of possible futures. The real question for us in the present and for historians thinking about any past present is this area of how do we understand the process of negotiation, which leads to choices of some narratives, therefore some futures rather than others. We simply do not understand that in any way. It is political. It is rhetorical. But we have no idea how to think about the nature of that kind of action and the constraints upon it.

FERNANDO GIL: Sometimes I think that complementarity might be a name for our ignorance. Is the community of physicists happy with expelling the idea of the longing for determinism?

AVIV BERGMAN: It's a nonquestion for us, at least for me, to think about what I do as a practicing biologist in terms of whether my actions would bring me closer to deterministic explanation or phenomenon. Biology is a very automatic field because it is composed of two, in a sense, separate fields. One is functional biology, which is closer to the physical sciences where determinism might play some sort of a role. The other side of biology is the historical side. This is evolutionary theory. Evolutionary theory is an historical science in nature. And biologists have a hard time separating those two. If you set your mind to understanding evolutionary theory and functional biology as a science that cannot be addressed as a physical science but as something which is a quite unique, then I am completely happy about the social question of ending the issue of determinism because by including the historicity of things into the equation, it becomes a nonquestion. So I am doing experimental science by studying the functional element of it but I am bringing evolutionary thinking to the field.

V. BETTY SMOCOVITIS: The most sophisticated person who's dealt with these issues of contingency and historical contingency is Richard C. Lewontin. Of course, Jared Diamond is also an evolutionary biologist, he is a physiological ecologist who's worked down in Melanesia, and I look at that book and I see such historical determinism, biological determinism, and yet he used it as liberating at the very end. And here is another way that he is escaping dealing with a kind of a deterministic universe. And there is Edward Wilson, *On Human Nature*. If you follow the logic of his argument about genes in society you are going to end up with a kind of determinism, but he does not believe it. There is room for free will and agency; it is one of these dilemmas that he writes about. I'm wondering if there is some kind of generational component here because Wilson, Paul Erlich, Gould, all the people that I have in mind are in their sixties and seventies and they came of age in the 1960's and they were sort of the same people who had the exchange with sociobiology in the 1970's. I wonder if there is a kind of generational divide because I certainly do not see it as a worry in my colleagues in the biological sciences. I see people engaging in what looks like evolutionary psychology or sociobiology. And I am more reflective. I start getting uncomfortable. I think about what they are doing but it does not seem to trouble them, and these are politically engaged individuals, the younger people that I work with. So I am not quite sure if there is some kind of a generational component here to the way that biologists deal with these issues. I do think of biology as traditionally picking up on Ernst Mayr and some of the philosophers of biology who laid the groundwork for the field; they argued that it was the central science. If we go back to the positivistic ordering of knowledge looking at the disciplines of knowledge, biology is the central science. It is what connects the social sciences to the physical sciences. It is where we might expect to find debate about determinism; I mean this is on human nature, but right now if you look at the conversation, it is just not there.

DAVID BYRNE: The classical world had an archetypical story of imminent fate. You know things are going to be determined. And if you look at the tales and sagas of the barbarians, they are all about really important decision-making actors who take actions of which they bear the consequences which are willed by themselves. Epidemiological case history ties into some of the things you're saying because it's that branch of biology which is about the ecological story: the contingency of why that human ecology is working out like that and why another one is working out in a different way. It is that kind of description that seems to be important. You have very different trajectories that have occurred. We have a reasonably good idea of what has happened in Brazil, which unlike South Africa is not riddled with AIDS as the World Bank predicted in the 1980's. And that is a kind of determinism, but it's not the simple determinism of what will happen or will not happen. It takes us right back to my archetypes because that is where actors and agents opted in particular ways.

ELIZABETH (BETSY) ERMARTH: I am also interested in this problem of common language that Alexei mentioned. It is very depressing to think that we are sort of trapped in this historical method, but I certainly think it is so in the humanities. I do not know what is humanistic about them although we seem to have this sociological quasi-scientific historical apparatus that is inescapable. And so I think maybe what we should be talking about here is disciplinary determinism because the disciplines in academia consign you to a certain language, a certain methodology no matter how courageous and strong and determined you are. They are very powerful and that seems to be a major subject for people who are interested in crossing. And I have been doing it all my life, my career. So I know it is fun but I also know it is very hard to find an institutional home for the kind of crossings and the kind of methodological comparisons that we are beginning to do here today. So I think that history, at least in my corner of the universe, is the culprit, which is why Foucault was so instrumental, so effective because it is at least the tectonic rather than that evolutionary idea which is fairly modern.

ALEXEI GRINBAUM: Complementarity is a crucial point. It is of course very comfortable to think about complementarity as just ignorance: We have not done enough research, so we do not know. That is not true, that does not work. Complementarity is a fundamental feature in physics. It is not just that we do not know and someone else knows, but that it is impossible to know. Complementarity means that the only way to give a complete description of the phenomenon is to give a set of complementary incompatible descriptions, each of which says something about the phenomena, but they are not compatible with one another. To look at this at a very general level and as a sort of theory of systems, if the system has been told where you are going to end up and the actor is within the system, then the actor acts so as not to get there. But of course the actor from within the system cannot self-predict fully. That is why there is this impression of determinism because it is sort of external. I just wanted to bring up this issue of prediction from inside the system, self-prediction, and this kind of determinism, of an agent who is not an external agent but who is an actor at the same time.

JOÃO CARAÇA: Now the question of complementarity, as Bohr put it, is well-adapted to the problem of wave and particle description. Wave and particle are a bit deterministic because wave is looking at the future; it is the way matter propagates. And particle is looking at the past, the way it interacts and we have information afterwards. That is why I prefer the words, but then again a word is a trap, right? Incompatibility shows better the essence of this subworld, the world of particles. It is in fact an incompatibility between certain categories.

IMMANUEL WALLERSTEIN: Incompatible is a kind of negative term. Complementarity is a kind of positive term. One is looking at it as a virtue, the other is looking at it as an obstacle. It may be the same thing.

BOAVENTURA DE SOUSA SANTOS: I would like to take a long duration perspective on this: is science becoming more experimental or more speculative? That is to say, are we going in the direction in which less testable science is possible in spite of what Aviv [Bergman] is telling us, particularly in physics? Is it becoming more speculative? This should have a kind of interesting consequence for social action because I see a disjuncture here. On the contrary, social action is becoming less speculative and more experimental, that is to say, the crisis of the philosophies of history—Marxism is one of them—shows that we are becoming much more experimental and less speculative. If that is the case, then, my kind of past is future-oriented always. My question is how to define this bundle, which we could call the horizon of determination, that is some possible futures? Here then it is a field of action and that is why experimentation is fundamental. It explains the question of why South Africa went one way and Brazil went another way because Brazil decided in favor of a simple thing—free access to drug therapies to everyone with HIV and the production of generics. That was the deal. That was the trick. For some time South Africa did as Mbeki said—label AIDS as a Western conspiracy against South Africa. That is why there is now an epidemic in South Africa and Botswana and there is not one in Brazil. There were crucial experimental and political decisions and actions that in fact could create these alternative futures.

HELEN LONGINO: A couple of points: One has to do with the parallels that we seem to make between certainty and determinism on the one hand and uncertainty and indeterminism on the other. We can lack knowledge about perfectly determinate processes so that our uncertainty is not the same as the indeterminacy of the processes. Regarding complementarity: the randomness that seems to be at the heart of physics is identified at one level of the physical universe, but at other levels of the physical universe we have what seem to be perfectly determinate processes. There are debates about what is the relationship between our classical descriptions and our quantum descriptions of the physical world. But there do seem to be perfectly determinate outcomes of actions of bodies at certain levels of description. So determinism has not disappeared from physics. That leads me, in an indirect way, to a point I wanted to make in relation to complementarity, that somewhere between certainty and uncertainty is the partiality of our knowledge, where we are someplace between knowledge and ignorance and we can have quite full knowledge but that is partial in its extent. That is, full in terms of knowing many of the details but revealing only a part of the phenomenon about which we are talking. Similarly, and that is related to another notion of totality or completeness, narrative always gives us a partial story. I also think the sciences that we have operating at different levels are giving us partial stories. There is a lot more to be said about that but if we think about the partiality of our knowledge, some of the puzzles about certainty and uncertainty, knowledge and ignorance, and also some of the puzzles about determinism and indeterminism, then we can understand how colleagues, who are not worried about determinism, are working at a certain level of analysis where these big stories don't matter. They can perfectly well do their work without the big story.

V. BETTY SMOCOVITIS: I want to echo what Betsy [Elizabeth Ermarth] was saying and maybe picking up on this idea of the narrative again. The "N" word is a very important critical word, and that is there are such things as unifying narratives that are reductionistic, that will streamline. One narrative that is very important and largely hidden from view is the narrative of the disciplines, the history of the disciplines of knowledge, which supports the view of the unity of knowledge and the idea that knowledge grows in what I call a dendritic growth process. I think it important for us to recognize and locate ourselves within that as we talk about our disciplines of knowledge because we have inherited from textbooks the way we have been disciplined to be either biologists or sociologists,

IMMANUEL WALLERSTEIN: I think it's time to give the floor back to our paper giver to comment on the comments.

STEVE FULLER: I want to make three comments. The first one is a general comment to take forward for the rest of the conference. We are talking very much at an abstract level of different kinds of models of how time is constituted. I wonder to what extent does any of this have a payoff for actual research practice in any particular discipline? I think philosophy is the natural home for this discussion. In a sense we have been having a philosophical discussion here this morning. But there is a question about the extent to which these models and these conceptions have any payoff for the more empirically-oriented disciplines. Or whether research just continues as usual, as it were, and then we sometimes spend time talking about this stuff in abstraction and we call it philosophy and we are doing philosophical research. This is something we need to take forward. When I wrote this paper I was actually thinking in terms of how does research practice change, particularly, historiography? How does that change if one thinks about determinism in a certain kind of way? And that was the way I addressed the issue because I took that to be in the spirit of this conference. But it is not just about the philosophical future of these concepts, but also their implications for research practice across various disciplines. That might be something to be brought out a little bit more in the conference. A more specific point. There was this issue of why physicists are not concerned about determinism today, and social scientists are? We might say that the aspect of determinism that was very important in the history of physics in the past is the philosophical aspect of physics that typically had something to do with God, and issues of agency and the relationship between the creator and the created. Those issues have dropped out of physics, so in that sense you do not actually need to talk about that any more. Nevertheless they do remain in the disciplines with a stronger philosophical residue, like the social sciences, which are still very much concerned with these matters. So I do not think it's any sign of physics envy per se. We have to realize that the history of physics originally contained this philosophical element which then was left behind. This element remained in the social sciences, and of course remains in philosophy. I do not consider it a particular disadvantage to the social sciences or philosophy that we are still concerned about determinism. The final point concerns why are not the young biologists worried about determinism? I think it is one of the things we really have not talked about; what is your paradigm case of determinism? What does determinism look like? One of them is the Laplacian image. But in biology there is a kind of very coarse-grained biological determinism that no self-respecting biologist of any branch of the discipline now adheres to, and it is: Oh, that is just from the bad eugenicist past or some other biological determinist past. And that is what these young biologists think determinism is or was. They do not see their own work that way because their own work is much more nuanced. It is based on a sort of probabilistic understanding of genetics in relationship to the environment and so they do not recognize determinism in any of that. They do not see the lineage. They think they are doing something totally different, that determinism is associated with just that kind of late-nineteenth, early-twentieth century view. There is a good point there, namely when one is rejecting determinism, one is often rejecting certain paradigm cases, but yet there may be residues of these positions still in one's own. We just do not recognize it.

IMMANUEL WALLERSTEIN: Are you saying that we throw determinism out the door but that it comes back in through the window?

STEVE FULLER: Yeah!

IMMANUEL WALLERSTEIN: So that determinism is a live continuing issue within biology, within physics, within everything.

STEVE FULLER: You'd better believe it.

JOHN MARTIN FISHER: I think we, in the social sciences and philosophy, have a kind of physics envy in the sense that we have an attraction toward determinism. The two reasons are that it is connected with explanation and it is connected with moral responsibility. On the one hand we tend to think we cannot fully explain an event unless we can give it some sort of deterministic explanation, or at least that is one kind of intuition or strand of thought that you cannot fully explain why something happened unless you can give it a contrasted explanation, you can explain why this happened rather than something else happening. On an indeterministic model it looks like you cannot give that kind of explanation. Now I think it is contentious whether you need that kind of contrasted explanation. I think also the same is true about moral responsibility. The criminal or the person accused of committing a crime in an indeterministic world can always tell the judge, "Look, I did rob from the poor box, but if we can roll back the universe in our minds to the past and let it play itself out and holding everything about the universe fixed, everything about me fixed, sometimes I will rob from the poor box and sometimes I will not in this thought experiment. And it is unfair to hold me accountable." In other words, there are very good responses to that kind of scepticism, but to put it simply, you raise the issue of physics envy and determinism envy and there is an ambivalence in philosophy because we do have an envy but we also have a fear of it. It is a threat to our free will. But I think the envy part comes from views about explanation which are contentious and worries about responsibility, which are also contentious.

IMMANUEL WALLERSTEIN: There is the ancient cartoon, which shows the criminal before the judge and he says, "Judge, you have got to be indulgent to me. I am the product of my biography." The judge says, "I am, too. Thirty years!" Let me say a word about physics envy. Physics envy is not merely an abstract intellectual concept. It is a very material, concrete thing. The crucial reason social scientists have physics envy is that physicists get a lot more money from society. We can trace for a hundred years and fifty years the social conquest of physics, of the natural sciences in general vis-à-vis all the other disciplines. Physicists have gotten more money and more social recognition because they have produced very concrete things which the larger society thinks are useful, such as telephones and airplanes. And what has an economist done lately except make a bad prediction about the economy? And what has a sociologist done lately except mumble something about whether criminals should or should not be treated harshly? And society does not really appreciate that very much. So we poor sociologists, we have envy because you get lots of money and lots of social recognition. I think we have to put that element into our analysis of what is going on here. It has nothing to do with whether we believe in determinism or do not believe in determinism.

SESSION II

MOBILE ORDER: BETWEEN CHANCE AND NECESSITY

Fernando Gil

I

To go back to the beginning: such is, after all, the charge given to the philosopher. I will thus attempt to clarify the network of meanings covered by
the terms "chance" and "necessity." These concepts were already opposed in early
Greek thinking, and Aristotle, who will serve as my constant reference in this paper,
thematized this opposition. It may indeed seem strange to place this discussion
under the sign of Aristotle, since the question of necessity, and even more so that
of chance, has been profoundly reformulated over two centuries by the modern
concept of probability, and then later by statistical mechanics and quantum physics, and, even closer to our day, by the ideas of order within fluctuations and the
theory of chaos. This is not even to mention the role of chance in avant-garde
art, music, and poetics.

Aristotle's treatment of chance and necessity shows us once again a distinctive
feature of philosophy: that the first statement of any major problem already contains the questions that will unfold in it as it develops historically. Of course this
can only be evaluated after such unfoldings have taken place, and this evaluation
entails the risk of retrospective illusions. Such is the danger of so-called "recurrent" history. My reading of Aristotle is somewhat anachronistic; it presupposes
the whole history of the concepts of chance and necessity. However, this is not
entirely the case, either. The difficulties—which as you know is the meaning of
the word *aporia*—that continue to frame, to constitute, and also to hamper our

comprehension of chance and necessity, already exist in Aristotle, who thus provides a useful starting point for our reflections. Chance and necessity form a true categorical opposition—which is anything but innocuous, for like other similar conceptual dualities, it involves a polarity that underlies our understanding of experience. The history of philosophy and science has confirmed Aristotle's claim, at the opening of the *Physics*, about the Ionian physicists, his predecessors: they take oppositions to be the principle of all things, "giving no reason indeed for the theory, but constrained as it were by the truth itself" (I, 5, 188 b 26–30).[1] Such binary thought, as Claude Lévi-Strauss has shown, runs throughout mythology. In Aristotle's direct line, René Thom maintains that a "constitutive aporia" guides each scientific discipline, for example, the difficulty of conceiving simultaneously the discrete and the continuous in mathematics. The "themata" studied by Gerald Holton exhibit quite clearly this same resonance of conceptual pairs in the history of science. One could provide other examples. We will simply add that although such oppositions raise barriers against intelligibility, categorical oppositions also offer opportunities to conceptualize. They open the door to a kind of research that is capable if not to overcome them, then at least to render them more manageable and intelligible. Such is the function of the "intermediary concepts" that will concern us here. The difficulty, the aporia, appeals to a "euporia," that is, the way out of an impasse. Scientific progress derives in part from this. In the first volume of *The Man without Qualities*, Robert Musil cites the following passage from Goethe that I have chosen for a title: "This beautiful concept of power and limits, of arbitrariness and law, of mobile order . . ." (*Dieser schöne Begriff von Macht und Schranken, von Willkür und Gesetz, von beweglicher Ordnung . . .*). To be able to conceptualize mobile order is the ambition of great philosophy.

I will leave aside the logical realm of necessity, as well as the logical relations between the necessary and the non-necessary. Several "nonclassical" logics have reworked the notion of necessity, including inductive logic, which, among other things, formalizes probabilities, which I will take up in a moment. Here, the relation of implication is partial; the conclusion does not follow from the totality but only from a "part" of the premises. If four-fifths of the cars registered in France were made in France, it is likely that my car (which was registered in France) was made in France. But in reality, it was not: the problem of inductive logic consists in determining the "degree of confirmation" of a hypothesis by a certain group of facts.

In Aristotle's time and likewise in ours, the concepts of chance and necessity govern *human action*—from history to morality. At the end of this paper I will apply these Aristotelian concepts to a corpus in which action is concentrated and intensified, so to speak, in the Goethean sense of the term intensification: the world of opera. In the *Nicomachean Ethics*, Aristotle opposes the uncertainty that characterizes action to the exactitude of "autarchic" or self-contained sciences, which are said to be governed by sole necessity (III, 3, 1112 a 17–b 11). Aristotle was wrong about that, as we know now. Chance permeates physics and biology, and it is the principle of "stochastic" music. This error only renders more pertinent the following proposition from *De Interpretatione*: "perhaps, indeed, the necessary and the not necessary are first principles of everything's either being or not being" (13, 23 a 19–20).

To be more precise, this passage from the *Nicomachean Ethics* distinguishes the domain of *action*, where deliberation takes place—and therefore choice, as we learn later on—not only from the *uniformity* proper to necessity (uniformity of eternal things, certain natural facts and autarchic sciences) but also from *chance, tyche* (for example, the finding of a treasure chest). Rational deliberation and choice are "in our power"; chance and necessity are not. As for action itself, when we put this text next to others, notably book 2 of the *Physics* (II, 5–6, cf. 197 b2), it appears that action constitutes, all things considered, a mixture of chance and necessity. Aristotle does not say this outright but it is as though absolute necessitarianism is as unintelligible as pure chance. Jumping forward in time, we might say that the lesson of Leibniz's doctrine of necessity is not far removed.

I will have to neglect certain important aspects of the Aristotelian theory, notably his consideration of two forms of chance: that is, "chance" or the "haphazard," *tyche*, and the "automatic" or "spontaneous," *automaton* (in French we normally translate *tyche* by "fortune" and *automaton* by "hazard"). This distinction is of small importance to our subject, and so we will consistently use the term "chance."

One may notice, first of all, that as opposed to necessity, chance is presented in a negative way, and will continue to be so presented up until the theory of probability. Aristotle does not attempt to define it, because it is beyond definition. Thus, it may appear to some as "inscrutable to human intelligence, as being a divine thing and full of mystery" (literally, a thing divine to a superior degree, *daimonioteron*, *Physics* II, 4, 196 b 6–7). Chance remains profoundly unintelligible, and nothing in its province may be explained. In fact, only the necessary and that which happens most of the time (*to pollu*) are able to be explained through demonstration (cf. *Post. Anal.* I, 30, *Physics* II, 5). The *Magna Moralia* formally exclude chance from the sphere of comprehension. "Where there is most *noûs*, there is least chance, and where there is most chance, there is least *noûs*" (II, 8, 1207 a 1–10). The *Metaphysics* Δ 30 explains that accidents (*to symbebekos*, perhaps better translated by "that which happens alongside")—for example finding a treasure chest when one is digging a hole for a plant—relates to something actual and is true, that is, real; but this is not due to necessity or to that which happens most of the time. The cause of the accident is indefinite; it falls into the domain of chance (1205 a 14–29). Accidents are partially related to chance. In consequence there could be no science of the accident, which moreover is close to nonbeing (*Metaphysics*, E 2, cf. 1027 a20 and 1026 b20). All in all, for Aristotle chance is the name given in common to the many figures of the non-necessary.

Chapters 4–6 of the second book of the *Physics* contain a close examination of chance. Aristotle poses straight away the question: *does chance exist?* "Some people even question whether there are such things [as *tyche* and *automaton*] or not" (195 b 36). Aristotle has Democritus in mind, but this problem, which is the fundamental metaphysical problem, remains fully up-to-date. Aristotle's response, or responses, seems to suggest the correct answer: that there is no true solution to the problem. It is still waiting to be solved. Among the chance situations imagined by Aristotle, the intersection of several independent causal chains, following a designation that has become popular at least since Cournot (cf. 1851, § 30) holds a privileged place. I will cite two instances, among many: "for example coming by chance into the market and finding a man there whom one wanted but did not expect to meet, is due to one's wish to go and do business in the market" (*Physics*, II, 4, 196 a 3 ss). One may extract from this an argument against the reality of chance (*Physics*, II, 4, 196 a 3 *ss)*. Likewise, "the stone that struck the man did not fall for the sake of striking him; therefore it fell by chance, because otherwise it might have fallen by the action of an agent and for the sake of striking" (*Physics*, II, 6, 197 b 30–31). Both the fall of the rock and the location, at a certain crucial moment, of the person it fell upon, have causes. These causes however are "exterior," Aristotle explains, and to this degree the events are the effects of chance (*Physics*, 197 b 18 ss.). But it might be observed that a better knowledge of the causes of such "accidents" as an unexpected encounter with someone or the falling of a rock on a passerby would permit us to determine why the two people crossed paths, why the passerby happened to be where he or she was at that moment and why the stone fell. According to this description, chance would reveal itself to be a surface effect. Thus, and against the main direction of his own thinking, Aristotle is obliged to recognize the accuracy of the thesis that "as an absolute (*haplos*) cause chance is not the cause of anything" (5, 197 a 14). Like probability, according to the proponents of the so-called "subjective" theory of probability, chance reflects our ignorance, and does not present an ontological truth. "Although there is some other cause, we do not see it" (*Eudemian Ethics*, VII, 14, 1247 b 5–10). In consequence, as Aristotle comments in a repetition of his *Physics* (II, 4), some people accord chance a genuine reality but one inaccessible to human thought.

In other words, the causality of chance would in the final analysis be *noumenal* (pardon this anachronism as well as those that are to follow). In absolute terms, the principle of sufficient reason demands the positing of a cause (*ratio essendi*). In "relative" terms—*which are at any rate those within which the human mind operates in its actual exercise*—one may never be certain to have achieved a full knowledge of that cause. (This is what finitude implies in Kant or Fichte.) And this is true, not "accidentally" but *on principle* (*ratio cognoscendi*), Aristotle suggests; and here his analysis is quite profound. It proves impossible on principle to climb back up the whole chain of causes that would explain an accidental event, because these causes are precisely "infinite (*apeira*) in number" (*Physics* II, 5 197 a 17). "The cause by itself is determinate; the accidental cause is indeterminate (*aoriston*); for an infinite multitude of accidents can result in a thing." The ever possible infinity of accidental causes—that therefore fall within the domain of chance—leads to an indetermination that in itself is *essential* and not accidental.

Among the multitude of causal antecedents, the circumstances of time and place (Aristotle says "now" and "here" in *Metaphysics* Δ, 30, 1025 a 20–26) are particularly difficult to tie into a necessary causality. In fact, in our examples the unforeseen resides less in the mere intersection of causal series than in the *simultaneity of the occurrences* "in a particular here and a particular now." Combining our two examples, we may conclude without great difficulty that the fall of the rock was set into motion by a gust of wind and that the passerby it hit was going to market to do business. But the overlapping or the coincidence *hic et nunc* of the two chains of events, arises from a network of determinations much more complex than the simple combination of the execution of the intention to go to market and an occurrence of the law of falling bodies. One would need to take into account why the passerby chose the path he took and why he moved at a certain speed, why he woke up when he did, and so forth, moving backwards through time—and also why the gust of wind arose at that precise moment, why the stone was where it was and why it could fall at that moment, etc. And yet all this would not completely explain the fact of the simultaneity. This is perhaps the reason that Aristotle repeats that "in consequence, there is no definite cause of the accidental, but a cause due to chance, and this is indefinite" (*Physics* II, 5 197 a 17, *Metaphysics* Δ, 30, 1025 a 20–26); it should be remarked that Aristotle comes back to this idea after his considerations of the "here and now" (*Physics* II, 5 197 a 17, *Metaphysics* Δ, 30, 1025 a 20–26). Like "objective" probability, the opacity of chance does not entirely avail itself to explanation.

It might be objected that nothing, however, prohibits a full knowledge of the total system and thus obtaining the full knowledge of the causes of an event. This may be so, but we should then agree on the meaning of "full knowledge." I submit that the alternative is undecideable, and Aristotle recognizes the plausibility of both theses. "For all these statements are correct, as might be expected. Things *do*, in a way, occur by chance, for they occur accidentally and chance is accidental cause. But chance is not the cause without qualification of anything; for example, the cause of a house is a house builder, and accidentally it may be a flute player" if the latter had designed the house (*Physics* II, 5 197 1 17). This is a matter much larger than the sole distinction between a "proper cause," "by itself," "absolute" (the architect), and an accidental cause (the flute player). Because it could in fact happen that the flute player and not the architect had been the creator of all of the houses in the city. Accidental causes may indeed be "infinite in number" (197 a 17, quoted above) and the determination of the cause "by itself" may therefore remain indefinitely adjourned. This Aristotle does not tell us, but his admission of accuracy "in a certain sense" of the noumenal thesis signifies no more and no less than this.

Lorraine Daston (1988), Ian Hacking (1975, 1990), and Ernest Coumet (in a number of articles), among others, have shown how probability theory and its developments, above all statistics—its "armed wing" (Ian Stewart)—have imparted consistency and substance to chance. Little by little it has lost its simply negative tenor, ontological as well as epistemological. Its "taming" by calculus transformed chance into a powerful tool of discovery and production of knowledge. During the nineteenth and the twentieth centuries probability and statistics have enriched the physical and the social sciences; they are at the core of insurance policies and opinion polls.

This has paradoxically conferred upon chance a new metaphysical preeminence. Probability is founded upon the so-called "laws of chance"; it represents the intrinsic legality of chance. There is a paradox in the sense that probability implies the recognition *both* of statistical regularities and aleatory indeterminism, or freedom—other names for chance—of the behavior of individuals. Ian Hacking draws attention to the importance of von Neumann's theorem of 1936 which intended to demonstrate the irreducibility of statistical laws to underlying non-probabilistic (determinist) laws. The trajectory of a particle can only be described in terms of probability (cf. Ian Hacking 1990, 116, 181). This would confer full ontological status onto chance, albeit relative. However, its intelligibility remains an open question; statistical regularities and liberty do not go hand in hand. Von

Neumann's demonstration has not convinced everyone. I will refrain from commentary in this matter, as it falls outside my sphere of competence. Its relevance was reinforced by chaos theory. In his stimulating work, Ian Stewart points out that, not only is chaos theory compatible with determinism, but it also allows individual quantic objects to be equipped with a determinist dynamics (1989, chs. 15–16) This theory would represent the fulfillment of the oxymoron, if I might say, of a "stochastic determinism": chaos partakes of both chance and necessity; it is an intermediary concept.

II

In Aristotle, chance is opposed to *necessity*, the habitual regularity of nature ("chance has no place in that which is natural, and what happens everywhere in every case is no matter of chance," *De Caelo* II, 8, 289 b 26), and to that which occurs *most of the time*; I will take up this idea of "frequency" in a moment. The non-necessary is comprised of randomness, indeterminateness, contingency, freedom, and of course possibility. This latter does not fall into the domain of chance. I will permit myself to associate randomness (or the aleatory) and indeterminateness to the degree to which the randomness constitutes, so to speak, the extreme form of indetermination (but indetermination is of course not always random). In fact, the purely aleatory is defined by uniform distribution and stochastic independence of occurrences, in the absence of reasons to the contrary. Together, these two principles form the "symmetry" at the base of classical probability theory. Since randomness strictly speaking plays only a modest role in Aristotle, I prefer to speak of indetermination.

A more or less significant lack of internal legality—or "conformity to the law" as Kant would say—characterizes all of the modes of non-necessity. In the quoted passage from *Magna Moralia*, chance signifies the opposite of the "order and uniformity" proper to the *noûs* (*mens*, intellectual intuition, comprehension). The

Eudemian Ethics poses chance as a cause "that is unseen" and Aristotle immediately evokes dice games (*alea* in Latin, cf. VII, 14, 1247 b 15–20).

I do not intend to inflict upon the reader the entire Aristotelian corpus on non-necessity, just a few brief indications. "Necessary" is opposed to:

1. The *contingent*, whose best description is perhaps found in *On Generation and Corruption* II, 11. As opposed to that which *is unable not to be*, there are things that do not necessarily come to be, things that may not be (337 b 1–13). Aristotle did not forge a technical term for "contingency," but he clearly has in mind the sense of the term used by Leibniz, that is, "that thing whose essence does not imply its existence." In the *Rhetoric*, Aristotle explains that, "so to speak." none of our actions is necessary (I, 2, 1357 a 22–26). The polar opposite of the contingent (here Aristotle says "chance"), the eternal, is governed by necessity (*De Caelo, Book II*); eternity ensues from absolute necessity (*On Generation* II, 11, 337 b 25–338 a 2).

2. The *possible*, presented in the *Prior Analytics* as meaning either randomness, when nothing causes a thing to incline in one direction or in the opposite direction, or "indefinite," that is contingent (that which can as easily be thus or otherwise), or finally that which happens most of the time but which is not necessary (I, 13, 32 b 4–13). The *Metaphysics* prefigures the Leibnizian definition: something is possible "every time that it is not necessary that its opposite is a falsity" (Δ, 12, 1019 b 22–30). According to Leibniz everything that does not imply a contradiction and that can thus be clearly and distinctly thought, but without implying its existence, is possible. It is interesting that this logical definition of the possible is found within the framework of the chapter dedicated to "power" and "capacity" (*dynamis*). The logically possible and logically impossible represent "another way in which things may or may not be endowed with capacity." It is as though the domain of logic were noth-

ing but the formal version of physical and biological power and lack of power. One may remark that in this book of the *Metaphysics*—which is a philosophical dictionary—the possible is not accorded its own chapter (as opposed to the necessary, which is given chapter 5).

3. *Freedom.* One of the meanings of "necessary" is "compulsion" (*to biaion*), that is, "that which obstructs and prevents a desire (*hormé*) or a choice" (Δ, 5, 1015 b 26 ss.). However, voluntary action (or an action whose principle of movement is to be found within the agent) is the contrary of compulsion (*Nicomachean Ethics*, III, 1, 1109 b 35–1110 a 4). Choice always results from a voluntary action (III, chs. 2–3) and everything that results from compulsion is involuntary (III, 4, 1135 a 31 ss.; cf. *Eth. Eud.*, II, 7).

4. The *indeterminate*—which, as we know, characterizes the causality of an accident. "Since causes of this kind are indefinite (*aorista*), chance (*tyche*) too is indefinite (*aoriston*)" (*Physics*, II, 5, 197 a 20). The same is true of the causality of the automatic (II, 6, 198 a 1–4).

I will add just a word about necessity itself, largely studied in the *Organon* and the scientific treatises of Aristotle. "To be necessary signifies the following: to be incapable of not being" (*Metaph.* Γ, 4, 1006 b 32), Δ 5 specifying that the principal sense of necessity, that all the others come down to, is: *impossible to be otherwise* (Metaph., 5, 1015 a 33). This will become Husserl's definition of the apodictic; and for Aristotle just as for Husserl, mathematical demonstration (*apodeixis*) is the model (Metaph., 5, 1015 a 33). Experience teaches us that the contingent, the aleatory, the path chosen by freewill, and the possible may all "be otherwise."

The following table (Figure 2.1) presents the main *intermediary figures*—which are chapter headings rather than concepts—between Aristotelian necessity and modes of non-necessity. They correspond to our logical intuitions and each one underlies a certain realm of knowledge.

Beyond the frequent and the "probable," which is primarily treated in the *Topics* (in fact it is the plausibility of the probable that interests Aristotle), it would be

Necessary	THE PROBABLE	Probability theory	Possible
Necessary	THE FREQUENT	Statistics	Contingent
Necessary	INCLINATION	Human sciences, ethics	Freedom
Necessary	THE SPONTANEOUS	Auto-organization, chaos...	Indeterminate

FIGURE 2.1   THE MAIN INTERMEDIARY FIGURES BETWEEN ARISTOTELIAN
NECESSITY AND MODES OF NON-NECESSITY.

possible to discover in Aristotle an understanding of inclination and of spontaneity that does not fully overlap with *automaton* (this term is often translated in English as *spontaneity*). But our real reference in this matter would obviously be Leibniz. In a certain way, his entire work aims to displace and to overcome the massive binary oppositions of Greek thinking. Leibniz looked for a *logic of probability, and of frequency* (we owe to the late Ezequiel de Olaso the first important interpretation of Leibniz in this sense). The concept of *inclination without necessity* guides his theory of liberty, as opposed to necessitarianism, be it Christian or Spinozist. And *spontaneity*, associated with a certain conception of "power" and "determination" (we read, for example, in the *Theodicy*, § 288: "spontaneity, with which we determine ourselves") is for Leibniz the right alternative to the endless conflict between necessitarian mechanicism and "vitalist" indetermination. "Determination," in its most general accepted meaning—since it has many—"is the state from which something follows unless it is prevented" (*De affectibus*, Grua, 526).

Probability theory succeeded in rendering scientific the treatment of the *probable*. Two main metaphysical questions, at least—those of Aristotle—may be posed on this point. 1) Does probability theory represent a true "taming of chance"? Are there "laws of chance" or must we rather say, quoting J. von Kries, that "the uncertainties that we obtain in the concerned domains [where probability theory applies] have . . . no other meaning than the following: even where the results depend on chance, the knowledge that we have of the relations between the "spaces of free play" (this is a translation of *Spielraum*, cited in Bouveresse 1993) frequently authorizes expectations that are extraordinarily certain. What characterizes the method by which we become the masters of chance in a certain way, resides precisely and fully in the systematic formation of expectations on the basis of the principle of "spaces of free play"; and probability theory, strictly speaking, is nothing other than the systematic calculation of the relations between "spaces of free play" (J. von Kries cited by Bouveresse 1993, 119–20). It would be a mistake to pretend that probability theory effects a true calculation of chance, for "the only thing that one may rigorously claim is that it calculates our expectations relative to random events and that in certain cases allows the formation of expectations at a very high degree of certainty" (1993, 199–20). Granted. But the problem, it seems to me, is not so easily solved. Indeed, the margins of freedom, the "spaces of free play," which, among other things, will guide our expectations and decisions, are formed on the basis, *and solely on the basis*, of the results previously obtained—those favorable "certain cases." Now, these results consist of distributions of events that do not depend upon any kind of expectations: expectations arise afterwards, and refer to future distributions. This brings us to the second problem. Are probabilities objective, "propensities" (Popper) that are inscribed in the order of things, or do they relate back to the state of our knowledge and our ignorance? Regarding the law of large numbers and another context as well, Ian Hacking (1975, 1990) and Jacques Bouveresse (1993) underscore that we are far from finding a definitive response to these questions. These questions reproduce the sticking points of Aristotelian chance.

Analogous considerations may be brought up for the *frequent* and statistics. Regarding the idea of *inclination*, I will only remark that psychology, sociology, and economics, whatever the school of thought (and not only in methodologies inspired by Dilthey), seek precisely to reconcile the necessity of scientific legality with the liberty of human agents. Even (in an outdated example) the "relative autonomy of the superstructure" in relation to economic determinism is the Marxist version of this proposition. From this point of view, one may say that the human sciences have given themselves the task of resolving the Kantian paroxistic antinomy of liberty and necessity.

Finally, the realm of the *spontaneous* comprises many of the principal findings and problems in the physical and biological research of the past few decades. I imagine that these will take a central position in our debates.

To conclude, we should remark that the different planes of the necessary and the non-necessary may overlap. Thus, the success of probability theory and statistics has caused them to be exported into the social sciences; Hacking's *The Taming of Chance* brings to light the different ways in which the relation between statistical regularities and individual liberty has taken central stage in the social theory of the nineteenth century (see among other things, ch. 20 on Durkheim's *Suicide*). Likewise, ever since statistical mechanics, these disciplines have become the most important strategy in the effort to conceive simultaneously the determinate and the indeterminate.

III

Aristotle, you remember, claims that "so to speak" (*eulogos*), there are no necessary actions—as opposed to the "statistical fatalism" that seized nineteenth-century imaginations. Hacking cites Quetelet: "one would say that free will exists only in theory" (1990, 116). Even still, if this determinism becomes the new guiding principle in social sciences, it does not efface the sensitivity to chance that seems to dominate a human condition having very little control over events. Chance also appears to dominate an *historical existence* conceived as the "invention of liberty," to take up the striking title of Jean Starobinski's book on the French Revolution. As never before, it becomes apparent that freedom of invention, the vagaries of the markets of money and feelings, conflicts of interest, quite often have chance at their bottom—and that they all give rise to chance-like effects. The nineteenth-century novel often made this its theme.

French pupils know—or knew—by heart Hugo's famous verses about Waterloo:

Suddenly, joyously, he says: Grouchy—it was Blücher.
The spirit changed sides, the fight exchanged its soul.
(Soudain, joyeux, il dit : Grouchy—c'était Blücher:
L'esprit changea de camp, le combat changea d'âme)
(Hugo 1932 XIII, L'expiation)

Napoleon awaited reinforcements. But the circumstances of "now" (*nun*) indicated by Aristotle, slowed Grouchy down, and the German general arrived first. According to competent scholars, from a strategic point of view, however, Napoleon's battle plan was excellent. At the beginning of *The Charterhouse of Parma*, the Waterloo wanderings of the poor man Fabrice symbolize this same powerlessness in the face of chance.

The force of chance is no less than "the force of destiny," and one can be found at the origin of the other: in Verdi's opera bearing this title (*La Forza del Destino*), the sequence of destinies arises from an "accidental" bullet. Alvaro kills the Marquis of Calatrava, Leonora's father, and Carlo, her brother, vows to avenge the crime. In fact, the shooting itself is an effect of chance. Like Grouchy, Alvaro, whom Leonora is awaiting, arrives late and therefore he meets the Marquis ("It is impossible that he will not come," exclaims Leonora's maid when she hears Alvaro's horse: she wants to believe in the *necessity* of his arrival.) The same pattern is reproduced several times, once with an explicit reference to chance. Carlo is saved from brigands by Alvaro who hears his call for help ("*aita!,*" Act III). He asks Alvaro, whom he doesn't know yet: "Tell me, then, to whom I owe my life?"—"To chance," the latter responds. They seal a pact of friendship, that is, they pledge themselves to recognize a certain necessity that would become the background of future heartrending experiences. They shake hands.

In *Un Ballo in Maschera*, another handshake, this time a "pure chance" encounter, also controls the entire plot. The witch Ulrica predicts to Riccardo that he will die by the hand of a friend. Riccardo asks his name, and Ulrica explains that it will be the one who shakes his hand next. Riccardo challenges, then, the present assembly: "Who among you has the courage to prove the oracle false? No one!" Renato, the best friend of Riccardo and the husband of Amelia, beloved by Riccardo, enters just at that moment, hears this last exclamation and cries, "Yes! I do." The tangle of reasons that determined the entrance of Renato onto the scene and his response are certainly "infinite in number," *apeira*, to return to the Aristotelian designation of the accidental. Later on a drawing of lots confirms the role destined by fate for Renato; he will kill Riccardo with a bullet in the back. Which he does, the night of the ball.

The *Queen of Spades* by Tchaikovsky puts into play an even more complex dialectic between chance and necessity. Necessity is manifested in Hermann's passion for gambling (and in Lisa's passion for Hermann). The "secret of three cards" would permit one to overcome chance and to win ("the taming of chance"). The ghost of the dead countess who had kept the secret when she was alive reveals the three cards to Hermann: the 3, the 7 and the ace. Hermann draws the first two, but instead of the ace he draws the Queen of Spades, a portent of death. Necessity (death) is not a consequence of chance here, rather it gives back to chance its own jurisdiction. The randomness of the game (the queen and not the ace) comes to contradict the false necessity of a magical wisdom (the pseudo winning formula hidden in the three cards). But randomness in its turn obeys the instructions of a higher form of necessity, which orders Hermann's death.

One should add that in all of these cases—Renato, Hermann, Carlo or Alvaro—in reality, destiny asserts itself from within. The "proper cause," "by itself," resides within the individual people and their relations. The witches and the cards are the "exterior" masks of the movement of human souls, and hurl them into love and death. Being compulsory, this movement distinguishes itself from *inclination* or *spontaneity*. One nice illustration of inclination in Verdi is Falstaff, who goes to the second meeting while knowing very well that he will be deceived again. "Va vecchio John, segue la tua via." Another would be the friendship and lucid fidelity of Posa to Don Carlo. As for spontaneity—that which will almost inevitably follow unless it is prevented—spontaneity is the modality of non-necessity that commands the soul's motions in Verdi, Tchaikovsky and *tutti quanti*. Tatiana says exactly this to Onegin in her letter.

Other icons of necessity have an identical function. The witch of *Un Ballo in Maschera* gives Amelia the recipe for a magic potion that is supposed to make her forget her guilty love for Riccardo (as a forgetfulness potion brings Siegfried to renounce Brunhilde); Tristan and Isolde drink a love potion that Isolde thought was a death potion or poison. Love and death belong to the same register. As in Wagner's operas—the *Leitmotiv* is a musical icon of necessity or, rather, an icon of one identity that is necessary, a "fate motif" is heard several times in *La Forza del Destino*: in the overture, before Leonora's great aria in front of the monastery where she is seeking refuge ("Madre, pietosa Vergine"), at the end, after Alvaro and Carlo's duet that ends in their duel, and before Leonora's last aria ("Pace, pace, mio Dio"). Their destinies are played out in them.

In a certain way, nineteenth-century opera maintains the balance between necessity and the Aristotelian types of non-necessity: contingency, indetermination, freedom. (The possible, which is non-necessity without relation to chance, has no place in opera either). In the eighteenth century, the "game of love and chance" of the theater and opera does not signify contingency and indeterminacy. Well on the contrary, the *quid pro quos* and the mistaken identities of characters, that are the substance of these games, derive from the decisions of well-identified agents and even a game master (Don Alfonso in *Cosi Fan Tutte*). Little by little destiny ceases to be the *fatum* that controls life, and it appears rather to be the result of local determinisms—situations and configurations in which the agents find themselves inscribed—that crisscross the permanent possibility of the unpredictable.

It's remarkable that even the last of these monuments to necessity, by which I mean Wagner's *Ring*, attests to this inflection. With the death of the gods opens the possibility and the impossibility of human love, ecstasy and renunciation: perhaps here is the realm of the *possible*, which for human action gets mixed up with the indeterminacy of promises and the future. Alberich and Hagen, Wotan, Siegfried, Brunhilde, and the others contribute, gloriously or in a way unknown to them, to create that destiny that the Nornes think they are spinning at the opening of the *Götterdammerung*. Everything happens by way of humanity and human passions, here and now. Wotan and a mortal woman gave birth to Siegmund and

Sieglinde, the parents of Siegfried; Brünhilde disobeys Wotan and comes together with Siegfried. The ring of the Nibelungen—another icon of necessity—will be returned to the Rhine maidens. The entire *Ring* cycle is, so to speak, contained in the succession of motifs in "Siegfried's death march." The motifs of Wälsung, heroism, the sword, Siegfried, the hero, etc., brought together, are submerged in the death motif. But this latter in its turn cedes to the motif of Brünhilde—to freedom and love and to a transgression which is undetermined, that is, not foreseen by Walhalla's law.

In the twentieth century, *chance* will come into its own. Ligeti's *Le Grand Macabre* might be seen as its allegory. At the end of a tumult of comical and ludicrous situations—that is to say *improbable* situations—after a lack of determination of consequents by antecedents, in the atmosphere of a total contingency and liberty that bathes the whole opera, Nekrotzar, the grotesque prophet of the world's necessary death at the stroke of midnight, *is the only character that perishes.* Here is Ligeti's final scene indication: "The sun slowly rises. Nekrotzar remains motionless a moment and then slowly begins to shrivel up, getting smaller and smaller, transforming into a kind of ball, and finally disappears melting into the earth." Exit necessity; and the space of the aleatory opens.

NOTES

1. Citations of Aristotle are taken from Jonathan Barnes, ed. 1984. *The Complete Works of Aristotle*, rev. Oxford trans. 2 vols. Princeton: Princeton University Press, Bollingen Ser.

REFERENCES

Barnes, Jonathan, ed. 1984. *The Complete Works of Aristotle*, rev. Oxford trans. 2 vols. Princeton: Princeton University Press, Bollingen Ser.
Bouveresse, Jacques. 1993. *L'Homme probable: Robert Musil, le hasard, la moyenne et l'escargot de l'histoire.* Paris: Editions de l'Eclat.

Cournot, Antoine A. 1851. *Essai sur les fondements de nos connaissances et sur les caractères de la critique philosophique.* 2 vols. Paris.

Daston, Lorraine. 1988. *Classical Probability in the Enlightenment.* Princeton: Princeton University Press.

Hacking, Ian. 1975. *The Emergence of Probability: A Philosophical Study of Early Ideas about Probability, Induction and Statistical Inference.* Cambridge UK: Cambridge University Press.

——. 1990. *The Taming of Chance: Ideas in Context.* Cambridge UK: Cambridge University Press.

Hugo, Victor. 1932. *Les Châtiments.* (Orig. 1853). Paris: Hachette.

Musil, Robert. 1955. *The Man Without Qualities,* trans. by Sophie Wilkins, Burton Pike. New York: Knopf.

Starobinski, Jean. 1964. *Invention of Liberty, 1700–1798,* trans. by Bernard C. Swift. Geneva: Skira.

Stewart, Ian. 1989. *Does God Play Dice? The Mathematics of Chaos.* New York: B. Blackwell.

DISCUSSION

DAVID BYRNE: The word I seized on is stochastic. Yes, it is generally used as a synonym for randomness, but etymologically it is not. I think that's really quite interesting. As I understand it, correct me if I'm wrong, it has something to do with arrows.

V. BETTY SMOCOVITIS: Target.

DAVID BYRNE: So a stochastic process is something which is random but on its way to arriving somewhere. I thought that was really quite important in relation to your discussion of the stochastic cult, especially in terms of the theories of probability which I think are important.

JOHN CASTI: I want to relate back to the issue of looking at something from the inside as opposed to the outside, this sort of endo- versus exo- because it also relates to languages and metalanguages. How does the system look when you look at it from the inside and you discover there are certain things that just cannot be said? It is not that they are uncertain; they are just undecideable, literally undecideable. But as soon as you jump outside the system this undecideability vanishes. You see these are true statements, but they are unproveable from inside. And you see this distinction not just in mathematics; it is in biology, too. The single most characterizing feature of a complex phenomenon is emergence; how something like chaos, which is by traditional classical standards an absolutely deterministic rule-based process, can give rise to something that looks random from the outside. You don't know what the mechanism is that is generating the behavior of this process; it looks statistically indistinguishable from a—I won't say stochastic—random process. And how can that be if we do not have both language versus metalanguage inside and outside? How do systems when they are put in interaction generate new properties that are completely unpredictable from the known properties of the component systems? Hydrogen and oxygen, for example, put them together and you get something completely different than the components themselves. I think this is a very important phenomenon in the generation of the seemingly uncertain or unknown from completely classically deterministic activities, processes.

There are a lot of systems around that are unstable. They do not have to be chaotic in order to be unstable. The fact is that small changes can give rise to big changes in the outcome. But this is itself, in my view, rather closely related to phenomena of emergent properties.

JEAN-PIERRE DUPUY: They are unstable but they are deterministic.

JOHN CASTI: Deterministic, exactly in a very strong classical sense.

ALEXEI GRINBAUM: I have a problem with the attribution of specific functions of probability specific to freedom; you define it as choice, resulting from voluntary action where voluntary action means an action whose principle of movement is to be found within the action. While human sciences and ethics certainly take interest in such matters whose principle and movement is confined to the agent, this is not the whole story. Ethics must be interested as well in what you call contingency. The contingent according to the Aristotelian definition is a thing which has not necessarily come to be or which may not come to be. Now consequentialism bases moral judgments on the consequences of one's action. As far as this action itself is concerned, one is dealing with the notion of freedom. However, the moral consequentialist judgment comes after the action has been accomplished because it is based on the result. So freedom is no longer there. We naturally attempt to concede that freedom is not applied to past actions, which become pure facts. So once it is in the past, even God cannot change it. Now contrary to freedom, contingency did not disappear with the passage of time. If an event was judged contingent at some instance, T, it remains so at a later moment. Then this can be discussed, but consequentialism in ethics is based not in the consideration of freedom of an agent but because the freedom is no more, it cannot respond to considerations which are now meted out by all parties involved. If the consequences of the action are, for example, bad then the agent will be judged negatively based on these bad consequences. The judgment will appear to the agent, however, to be contingent, random because it was impossible for him to foresee all the causes that had led to the bad result.

DAVID BYRNE: I just want to go over this idea about necessity as you [Fernando Gil] presented it. It struck me that in this particular statistical model called Markov chains, what happens is absolutely dependent on what has happened immediately before. This is something which is used extensively in evolutionary studies, in genetics—the way in which they determine the particular sequences of genes. Here it is a necessity which is imposed but it becomes immediately random. The Markov chain seems to have embodied within it both the idea of necessity and the idea of randomness. So that what has happened is the precondition of everything that has happened subsequently. But that itself is strung on and on.

JOHN CASTI: I think that even with the quantum knowledge we have today, it would not be possible to understand the quantum structure of the hydrogen atom and oxygen atom and say that if I put these two flammable gases together then I am going to get a compound that puts out fire, a compound that is completely different in fundamental properties than its constituent parts. A more interesting example actually would be something in the social engineering domain, such as road traffic. Traffic jams are an emergent property and you cannot look at any individual car on the road and say there is a traffic jam there. It emerges out of the interaction of all the vehicles. It is the same with a price change in a financial market. That is a collective emergent property of the actions of all the individual traders doing whatever it is that they are doing and interacting. Or points scored in a football game—it is an emergent property of the individual objects making up the system. This is one way that I could say that you could reconcile the idea of having a completely deterministic mechanism, if you will allow the word, and still have a system that produces behavior that is unpredictable. To go from one level to the next relates to how we conceptualize the world. What are the concepts we are using? For hydrogen and oxygen gas there are a certain set of concepts that are appropriate for gases and if you put them together you have a new property which emerges, liquid, nonflammable. And you ask where does that concept come from? You cannot see that concept. Even if you know everything about hydrogen and oxygen gas, you are describing everything at a certain conceptual level. And when you put them together, I do not think the laws of physics are going to give you that concept.

JOÃO CARAÇA: I think it will be interesting to distinguish between two things, chaos and complexity. They are not the same thing. When we talk about chaos theory we are talking about nonlinear things, nonlinearity, which in the languages of the social sciences translates into interactions. So chaos is a creation of nonlinearity, which means interaction, so second order and things like this. Complexity is the difficulty of disaggregating a system from its environment, from the whole. That is to say, in the language of systems, complexity arises from the need to consider open systems. For instance, a living being creates its own environment. Where is the border, the boundary, between individual and the environment? It is really indeterminate; we do not know. This is the genesis of complexity. From this we see that different ways of looking at the problem can bring forth emergent properties or not. It depends on the level at which one is looking. In terms of the fundamental question, complexity brings another category here to our table that is not in Aristotle.

FERNANDO GIL: No, it is not.

STEVE FULLER: I guess this is going to be another remark about something that is not in Aristotle or at least I am not sure if it is in Aristotle and this relates to the way you [Fernando Gil] discuss necessity in your paper. It seems to me that Aristotle does not have a law-like notion of necessity, in the sense of modern physical law that is related to determinism. Sometimes the way you use the word regularity and the way you use this notion of conformity to the law strikes me as anachronistic because Aristotle's notion is closer to something like destiny—what naturally happens, without the notion of physical law where something has to be in place first before something else can happen. I normally think about this as a kind of Newtonian physical law type of determinism, which is quite a different notion of determinism than Aristotle's notion of necessity.

FERNANDO GIL: The content I give to necessity in Aristotle apart from logical description is what I call necessitarian determinism and I think it does correspond to the content of Aristotle's physics or biology when it speaks of necessity. I am deliberately using an anachronism.

JEAN-PIERRE DUPUY: There is the equivalent of a causal determinism that Aristotle called automaton, except we translate it as chance or randomness, because automaton for Aristotle's physics means pure causal determinism.

ELIZABETH (BETSY) ERMARTH: Aristotle's idea of causality is quite different from modern causality, as I understand Aristotle. There are four kinds of causes and they come in different sequences and they represent the flowering of an essence, not the sort of horizontal emergent form which may or may not be essential of causality and later modern description; so it seems to me that even the idea of causality is a different idea of causality than we would have.

JEAN-PIERRE DUPUY: Efficient causality in Aristotle is the closest to our concept of causality, but it plays a minor role in Aristotle. It is the final causality, as we know, *Telos*.

FERNANDO GIL: Formal causality is what we call formal constraints, laws of structure. Aristotle identifies it. Then there is the fourth, which is not a cause, which is the material substratum, but you know at least efficient, formal, and final causes have equivalents for us; they are still working with other names.

DAVID BYRNE: I continue to pick up your sentence on the first page [referring to Fernando Gil's paper], the way you presuppose the whole history of probability, chance, and necessity, and a couple of things occur to me. One, I think that the way the social sciences and the ecological and biological sciences use probability is quite different from statistical kinds. Statistical mechanics describes single systems. It reduces what is going on into a law; it translates all those kinds of things into a law. But statistics is always about entities, about what would happen across the whole population, about events. The uncertainty is not to touch any one of those entities but the description of the relationship of population and the entities. The second thing is, since we started talking about emergence, the method in which we see emergence in a way is simulation. And there are two kinds of simulation. One is very deterministic, which is the completely ruled kind of simulation. Right side rules and other things, so it is a bit like kids in the sense that chaos is about indeterminacy of measurement. It strikes me that this is what we have because I see that interruption in statistical numbers is a rather different thing. But the other kind is quite interesting. To make simulations work—I think Peter Allan does it, and every one of Prigogine's pupils, for example, pick up on that idea—to make the simulations work which are based on stochastic calculus, you have to write in somehow a randomness or white noise that shakes the thing, that kind of drives the system along. I think it is quite interesting if we see simulations as a way of representation, because it is not used extensively as an alternative to the kind of predictive law.

HELEN LONGINO: It seems to me that one of the notions that is left out, which we can see by focusing on the frequent, is universality. There are times when universality is confused with necessity. Newton's laws are intended as universal, that is, they hold for all bodies at all times, everywhere. But it is not clear if they have the same kind of necessity, or if they have any necessity, what kind of necessity they have.

IMMANUEL WALLERSTEIN: Could not they be universal if they were not necessary?

HELEN LONGINO: Why not? Sure. If we go back to this notion, it depends on what we mean by necessary.

IMMANUEL WALLERSTEIN: It depends on how universal it is.

HELEN LONGINO: If we go back—touché. But if we go back a bit, the impossible could be otherwise. If that is the meaning of necessity, then what is universal would be impossible to be otherwise?

JEAN-PIERRE DUPUY: Pi could be otherwise.

HELEN LONGINO: Yes.

JEAN-PIERRE DUPUY: Well, that is debatable.

HELEN LONGINO: If we set Pi within a system of mathematical understanding, then it seems less likely that it could be otherwise because we have no way of conceptualizing it's otherwiseness because we are already committed to it's being the way it is.

STEVE FULLER: Maybe this is fleshing out where Immanuel [Wallerstein] is coming from. I suppose universal and necessary are interrelated if you imagine universal across all possible worlds. If that is how you imagine physical law, I guess that is how you would get to his intuition.

BOAVENTURA DE SOUSA SANTOS: But what would happen if we started with the intermediate concerns and let them become the original concepts? What kind of backward, forward concepts will they create?

IMMANUEL WALLERSTEIN: What would happen if we started with the inter-mediate terms? What we basically have are what we normally start with, either necessity versus chance or the universal versus the particular, or a pair we have not mentioned so far, which is nomothetic/idiographic. These are the standard antinomies. None of them are intermediate terms. All of them are antagonisms or antinomic. Suppose we started with the four intermediary terms that Fernando Gil gives us, the probable, the frequent, inclinations, and the spontaneous, and then thought of what their antinomies would be. The antinomy of the probable is the improbable. The antinomy of frequent is the infrequent. It is a question of our basic approach to thinking about reality, the world, everything. We have always been thinking, it seems to me, in terms of system/chance, or universal/particular, or nomothetic/idiographic and these are incompatible. You are either one or the other all the time and then you worry about how that fits in with reality and this whole paper is an exercise in showing that it never is quite any of those, so let us find some intermediate terms. Maybe we should just stick with the intermediate terms and try to build all our constructs around them. What would then happen? I can see how I can do this in social science, but I do not know if it can be done in biology or physics—what one would do to build a physics around the probable versus the improbable, etc.

FERNANDO GIL: Everybody obeys necessarily the law of falling bodies, for instance. So you find necessity inherent to Newtonian mechanics, it seems to me.

HELEN LONGINO: Well, I'm not sure you find that you need necessity in Newtonian mechanics. All you need really is universality.

FERNANDO GIL: I'm not saying you need it: it is there in fact.

KEITH BAKER: I would like to interject a purely historical note. Newton did not believe the laws he described were necessary. This is an example of laws that were universal, that were not necessary. They were universal because they applied everywhere. But they were not necessary because God could change them at any moment. It seems to me that another aspect of this question is this issue between determinant and determined. Determinant is something that can be described precisely. There are determinant relations which we can express with precision. That has nothing at all to do with determination. The opposite of the necessary is the non-determinant. It seems to me the problem with this discussion is indeed that we are constantly mixing up epistemological statements and ontological statements—not surprisingly because Western thinkers have been doing this for at least 2000 years. It is also the problem with starting with the intermediate terms. We cannot start with the intermediate terms because they are merely intermediate. What is the opposite of the probable, the uncertain? What we would find is that there would be many possible pairs within these intermediate terms. It would be very difficult for us to decide on which to agree.

IMMANUEL WALLERSTEIN: But you are undoing what I tried to do.

KEITH BAKER: I know I am.

IMMANUEL WALLERSTEIN: You can start with any pair of terms because they are no longer intermediate terms at that point. You have the start, you have the original terms and if you make the opposite of the probable, the certain, or the frequent, the always occurring, then you are getting away from my whole attempt to create a pair of terms neither of which would in our normal language sound like an absolute term: the probable, the improbable, the frequent, the infrequent, the inclined, the disinclined, the spontaneous, the planned. None of them are absolute terms as we usually use them in the language. That would be a different epistemological approach to reality than the one we have been using for 2000 years—all these that we have been reminded of in this survey of Western philosophy that Fernando Gil has given us, which is absolutely correct. This is the way the philosophers and all the other scholars have approached the epistemological problem. Regularly they have all come up with the fact that reality does not quite fit in those antinomies and they are always worrying about how they can fit the two together, how you can be at one and the same time necessary and still have free will, and so on. That is because we started with terms which are impossible terms. We start only with things that are towards one end of a continuum versus towards the other end of the continuum, but not at the ends of any continuum. We build our whole way of doing history, of doing physics around that, but it doesn't fit the real world somehow. We somehow have to be Ptolemaic and get a little extra loop somewhere that will explain the curious deviation from what we observe from our theory.

DAVID BYRNE: Suppose we said, instead of frequent and seldom as an antinomy, always, frequent, seldom, never. We have four values. Most of the statistical reasoning in the social sciences which is not about inference from someplace is actually about degree of frequency because it is about core variation. It is about how often these happen together. Always and the never as opposed to the frequent and the seldom is one of the problems that we're trying to deal with. I agree frequency and contingence are what come in. This is where the whole idea of statistical interruption played because that is not how more things in play modify the relationship. The rules are very dumb, they change, they are specific depending again on a very important term that is brought in, free play, which I equate with the statistical term degrees of freedoms and ways of thinking about what we're doing.

JEAN-PIERRE DUPUY: I was very much interested in your conceptual strategy [referring to Fernando Gil's paper], which is opposed to what I am used to in philosophy. Your strategy is very well summed up by the title *Mobile Order*. You take seriously the fuzziness of those concepts. The strategy I have been accustomed to is exactly the opposite. It is to sharpen each one of those concepts to bring out their contradictions and then to try to transcend the contradiction. It is a very different strategy. This second strategy is much more traditional than the one you are proposing here—and I think it is very important that you are trying this other strategy—but the usual strategy first would be to try to come up with pairs that really constitute antinomies. Necessary and contingent are incompatible. You should take necessary to mean true in all possible worlds and contingent to mean true in at least one possible world but not true in all possible worlds, or those two concepts are incompatible. If you take freedom to mean free will, that is, the capacity to act otherwise, then freedom is opposed to necessity. But necessary and possible in that construct are not incompatible. Necessary means true in all possible worlds. Possible means there is at least one possible world in which it is true. This is perfectly compatible. If you take necessary and indeterminate there are two things to be said here. First the one that Keith [Baker] said, namely that there might be a lumping together of determinant and determined. If you take determined, something can be at the same time causally determined and not necessary, that is a problem of compatibility. Consider that the action I am taking now is completely determined, that does not mean that it is necessary. This is not meant to be a critique. On the contrary, I want to bring out the originality of your approach which is really to take the irreducible fuzziness of concepts seriously.

KEITH BAKER: Newton is very sensitive to the charge that he is introducing necessity. The argument is that God is actually in there doing it all the time. We really think the Newtonian is really the Laplacian system of the world in which all of that stuff has been taken out.

JOHN MARTIN FISHER: Going back to Immanuel [Wallerstein]'s point, I think that whether all universal generalizations are necessary depends on what you mean by necessary and also universal. I think this is a question about whether the laws of nature are necessary. The model status of the laws of nature is really intriguing and difficult, and also highly relevant to the free will issues. But I am inclined to think we can say, what Keith [Baker] attributes to Newton, that the laws of nature are not necessary. We could say they are not metaphysically necessary and that we could have had different laws of nature. So there are possible worlds and logical space that have different laws of nature or God could have actualized different possible worlds in which there are different laws of nature. But in this world we can distinguish between universal generalizations that are nearly accidental and those that are law-like, the laws of nature. It is very difficult to separate the generalizations that are accidental from the ones that are law-like. It has to do with counterfactuals—the accidental ones do not support counterfactuals in the same way that the law-like do. So it turns out it is a generalization that all U.S. presidents have been males but certainly we want to say we hope that is not necessary. But if you put a piece of salt in water it will dissolve. I mean there are certain laws that support counterfactuals. If you accept that there is some way of distinguishing the necessary generalizations from the merely contingent ones, the question is whether that kind of necessity is consistent with free will or not. About freedom and determinism, I think incompatibilists tend to think of a kind of necessity that is involved in the laws of nature as pushing us or pounding us like a gust of wind. We have to obey the laws of nature almost like we have to obey the laws of government. We know we just have to obey, whereas the compatibilist tends to think of that necessity as much weaker, as not pushing us. So a lot depends on your view of the kind of necessity that is encapsulated or found in the laws of nature.

V. BETTY SMOCOVITIS: Thinking about Newton again, I think Keith [Baker] amended his original claim with Laplace and the comparative perspective between Laplace and Newton. My understanding was that Newton wanted a limited role for God. God would be an intervener whenever the anomalies appeared. Like someone who would repair a clock. Something you said initially made me think that you thought he had a more active role.

KEITH BAKER: That basically comes in the Clark-Leibniz correspondence. Clark speaking for Newton has this very active conception of the way in which God acts in the universe. It is not just that God tunes at the edges, but He really is in there, almost pushing and pulling, you might say.

JEAN-PIERRE DUPUY: Laplace was expounding a system to Napoleon. Napoleon said: "What's the role of God in your system, M. Laplace?" He said, "I can very well do without God."

IMMANUEL WALLERSTEIN: "I have no need of God."

FERNANDO GIL: Which is a Newtonian quotation.

IMMANUEL WALLERSTEIN: It is irrelevant what Newton thought because Newtonianism is there despite Newton. But we are missing something in this whole discussion. Necessity comes in its strongest form in monotheistic theology in which it asserts God is omnipotent. Therefore, in one sense God has total free will. He can do anything God wishes. But also that nobody can affect that because God is omnipotent. Now the strongest version of the omnipotence of God is in Calvinism. Calvin asserts that because God is omnipotent, He has decided definitively for once and forever who will be saved and who will not be saved. And nothing, absolutely nothing that anyone can do can affect that decision because otherwise we would be more powerful than God. Instantly he realizes that this is absolutely paralyzing. Because if, in fact, there is nothing we can do that can affect whether we are saved or not, then we are free to do anything we feel like because it has already been determined by God whether we will be saved. And so having created this impossible situation, with the concept of absolute necessity, he finds the little door out of it immediately. This little door is that we cannot affect God but we can have foreknowledge of what God has decided. And Weber analyzes this all in the *Protestant Ethic*. We can have foreknowledge; we can see that if you behave in certain ways, it is certain that God does not intend you to be saved. If you behave in the appropriate way, it does not mean you will be saved, but at least you are in the category of people who might be saved. Therefore, you now have a reason to act in that way. What happens is you get the perfect form of necessity and then you say it is impossible. We cannot use it. We cannot deal with it in the world we have to create. I am saying let us get rid of it. Let us get rid of it completely, absolutely.

JEAN-PIERRE DUPUY: Immanuel [Wallerstein], I fully disagree with you because what Weber shows is that everything occurred as if the Calvinists endowed themselves with a counterfactual power to determine or to change their predestination.

IMMANUEL WALLERSTEIN: No.

JEAN-PIERRE DUPUY: Yes, yes, yes!

IMMANUEL WALLERSTEIN: Not change their predestination. No, absolutely not. In other words Calvinists said that if our own beliefs are true, we have no way of controlling your behavior. And that was so horrifying that they found this back door in their own theory of foreknowledge which then allows the church to control human behavior. You cannot be a Calvinist if you think that anything you can do can affect God's decision.

DAVID BYRNE: I'm not sure about this because I agree completely about the Calvinistic point. It is interesting that with the exception of some extreme Calvinistic sects in Scotland, all the traditional Calvinistic churches have abandoned the doctrine of predestination. They have given it up. This idea that God could turn off the simulation and just press a button and everything would start again is a very powerful idea. So what we did is we separated theology and science, except we did not. It even goes on into the nineteenth century; the same ideas are quite important.

JOHN MARTIN FISHER: Maybe you [Immanuel Wallerstein] were not suggesting leaping to that conclusion, but I think you said something like we should just get rid of this notion of absolute necessity. I was just wondering why. Why can we not keep it as a kind of norm? I do not know anything much about ideal gas theory but I heard that you could study the phenomena not assuming that any actual gases are going to conform exactly to the laws, but they are there as a kind of idealization and we can study phenomena and they can be illuminated by their proximity. So why can we not keep necessity in that sense?

IMMANUEL WALLERSTEIN: In other words, nothing is ever necessary, but some things are almost necessary, 99%.

JOHN MARTIN FISHER: Maybe nothing is physical about it. I would hold up mathematics and logic as places where there could be a kind of necessity.

JEAN-PIERRE DUPUY: But I do not think necessity is a scientific concept. Determinism is a scientific concept. Necessity is philosophical because it has to do with other possible worlds, etc., counterfactuals. That does not have a real meaning in science.

AVIV BERGMAN: How would you characterize the scientific field of fuzzy logic in this case?

ALEXEI GRINBAUM: For any logic there is this well-known play that any metatheory is always based on classical logic. That is, if you are working with fuzzy logic, inside you have different notions but still at the metalevel you have all the same. In scientific model you can do whatever you wish. It remains a model. Why does it remain a model? Because there is a metalevel, which goes out of the model. There is first order metalevel which does not obey the rules of the theories.

JEAN-PIERRE DUPUY: Since Aviv [Bergman] put the question to me, I think that fuzzy logic has to do with indeterminacy, not with the lack of necessity. It is always the same, fuzzy logic is supposed to solve the heap paradoxes. One stone is not a heap. If you add a stone to a non-heap it is still a non-heap. Nevertheless a heap of stones is made of stones. Where do you draw the line? Fuzzy logic was invented to solve that problem, that paradox of indeterminacy, not lack of necessity.

BOAVENTURA DE SOUSA SANTOS: I think it was not by accident that God came into our conversation because that is really part of our 2,000-year history and I think we could pursue that a bit further. Starting again on the questions of the intermediate and not intermediate concepts: If you assume that concepts are anthropomorphic, that is to say they are metaphors of the human condition, then probably we could see that the intermediate concepts are the concepts of human beings as complete beings. While the antinomic concepts, or extreme concepts, are the realm of a God-like type of power. That is to say, it is proper of our human condition in the West that there is a kind of conceptual division of labor between us humans and gods. Human beings can think both about intermediate concepts and extreme concepts. But they can only act on intermediate concepts. So we act through the middle; we think through the extremes. That is the arrangement. That is why I suggested the proposition to start from the intermediate and then our task is to see whether these extreme concepts are empowering, or disempowering. In my view they have probably performed both roles.

FERNANDO GIL: I am very seduced by what you say. I see very well gods and the necessity sides. On the other hand, what or who occupies the possible contingent freedom of the intermediate?

IMMANUEL WALLERSTEIN: Let me pick up on that because I think you have to put this in the context of the history of the structures of knowledge. God was central to thinking in the Western world for a long time. What we call science today was a process of people emancipating themselves from theology bit by bit. Newton was not very emancipated but we get to Laplace who says "I don't need that hypothesis, sire." In emancipating ourselves from the theologians, that is, from a group of people who asserted that they primarily had privileged access to the truth, a group of people called philosophers, and then later scientists, said no, we can have direct access to the truth through these various other mechanisms. It was organizational in one sense. It was a group of non-clerics saying that they did not have to check out their truths with the clerics as though the clerics knew everything, because the non-clerics can go to the laboratory, they can do experiments, can do X and Y, can read archives, can come up with historical facts, and can come up with other truths without the clerics. That was an organizational change. At the intellectual level it was harder to make the shift. What we did basically was take theological ideas and translate them into secular equivalents; we claim we are not being theological but we still have a lot of the flavor of it. Since we are not theologians, and since we are not God, it is very important that we have got to stop trying to use either the appurtenances of God or the privileged access to God through revelation or whatever else. We have to use truly secular concepts. And that is why I am saying, get rid of necessity. Necessity is basically a theological concept. And it is not in the real world. Or if it is in the real world, it comes into the real world as an asymptote. It is an asymptote which we never reach. That was the point that John [Martin] Fisher was making. I'm perfectly willing to say I have lots of concepts that are asymptotes. I talk about sovereignty in the modern state system. I make the point in my writings and to the students that no country is or could possibly be sovereign within the interstate system. But sovereignty is a concept and some states are more powerful and some states are less powerful. That is, some have more of the appurtenances of sovereignty or less, but none has all of them and could not have it. Could not have it. So I'm perfectly willing to use the word, sovereignty. It is a sense of an absolute and has lots of features which I could then define. But then I have to say that about everything about the modern world or about other worlds. So I'm giving up the idea that anything I could do would ever approximate a statement of necessity. There is no way in which, as a scholar, I can in any field make a statement about the necessary. I think it is an important psychological and intellectual shift to give up the antinomy and to stay strictly in this range of possibilities that are in between the antinomic extremes as the nearest approximations of reality—not only that we can reach in the state of our present knowledge but that we can intrinsically reach. That is to say, I want to make the assertion and that is supposedly the most challengeable, that there is no way—it is not a matter of our ignorance—that we can be godlike and therefore we can never make statements about necessity now or in the future no matter how much further sophistication, technology, research, or anything else that we have; we just cannot do it. It is important for us to recognize that and not make that a foundation of our assertions.

JEAN-PIERRE DUPUY: I tend to disagree. I think necessity is part of human experience. There is a Marxist word for that actually, alienation. It is the experience. I think it is part of the human predicament, the experience of the tragic. The tragic comes from us but we take it to be an external force. This is not an invention of theology. Every myth is about necessity, except if you consider that mythology is part of theology.

IMMANUEL WALLERSTEIN: Necessity is a theological idea and if you want to cite Marx that would be a good example of the opium of the masses. You are saying that people—empirical statement—that across the world over time in many of the areas or almost all areas, possibly all areas, one does not know, that people have come up with versions of necessity as explanatory of their real situation.

JEAN-PIERRE DUPUY: Yes.

IMMANUEL WALLERSTEIN: And I am saying that we as scholars, if we imitate this, are creating absolute dilemmas for ourselves out of which we cannot get because they are not good explanations of reality. I thought that in that sense the scientific adventure was somehow to go further than the simple explanation that people came up with to explain real things in the world. Why was there a thunderstorm, why was there a flood, why do people die young? These are realities and people do come up with explanations. The explanations are not necessarily good ones. And it seems to me we have created conceptual frameworks which do not allow us to get out of that.

ALEXEI GRINBAUM: I think there is a different vision of the necessary which disagrees with this vision. It is a neo-Kantian vision which removes all the theological evidence and then the necessary can be viewed as a condition of possibility. It is a condition of possibility of a kind of an intersubjective communication because the problem with the intermediate terms is that they are intermediate. If someone wants to make a statement which is repeatable, reproducible, and comprehensible for another person, then it might be necessary, while this remains to be shown if there is a transcendental argument or not.

IMMANUEL WALLERSTEIN: I would not understand you if you said it is probable that X happens?

ALEXEI GRINBAUM: Yes, because no one knows what "probable" means. And then push this to the extreme in order to produce precise statements which everyone understands in the same way, because probable for me may be different. We know the experiments in popular psychology: Probable can mean 10% and it can mean 90%.

IMMANUEL WALLERSTEIN: That's right.

ALEXEI GRINBAUM: I think one could try to show that there is a transcendental argument saying that if one wants to make a statement which is understood in the same way by the different agents and subjects, then we end up with some precise statements like the necessary statements. Well, necessary can be understood also in the technical sense.

IMMANUEL WALLERSTEIN: Mathematics is not a statement about the real world, is it?

ALEXEI GRINBAUM: Right. But when I am saying transcendental argument I am not saying that those are statements about the real world. I am saying those are statements about what I say which the other understands.

IMMANUEL WALLERSTEIN: But in a sense, what you say is: the best place to look for the lost set of keys is under the streetlight because there is more light there. In effect you are saying to me that I can better communicate with somebody else if I make a statement which is possibly not true. But at least it is equally understood by the other person. And I am saying to you: make the closest statement you can to what is reality and I know I will not understand it perfectly because my understanding of the words will be slightly wrong but at least you are communicating about where the keys really were lost.

ALEXEI GRINBAUM: You know where the difference lies between what you are saying and what I am saying? I am not assuming the existence of reality. What I am assuming before I start saying things, is that there is a stream of phenomena for me as one agent as well as a stream for the other agent to whom I am saying the phrase. There is no one underlying reality. There are two streams. I want to say something about which only I can perceive so that the other one will understand as clearly.

IMMANUEL WALLERSTEIN: I am all for it. Go ahead, say it and it may end up being a statement that is probable that this happens, the probability to a point 8 [.8] when we make these kinds of statements in the social sciences. These are the covariations which David Byrne was talking about. I am engaged in this kind of debate all the time. Somebody comes along and says it's only 3% and I say it is as much as 3%. We can debate whether 3% is a remarkable amount or it's only 3%. There is a difficulty of communication because I take into account many factors—X, Y, and Z—which you ignore. You take into account W, P, and Q, which

I ignore. Maybe we will have to keep talking and you will pull out all your extra factors and I will pull out all my extra factors and we will get closer and then we will communicate better.

ALEXEI GRINBAUM: All I am saying is that if you want to neglect this, if you do not want to do this every time you pronounce statements, then you push toward the necessary.

FERNANDO GIL: It is absolutely true that eternal things, God and the celestial, both are necessary. You are entirely right. But it is also true, and I agree with Jean-Pierre [Dupuy], that immutability of death is anarchy. It is an absolute necessity. Then you have something which is for Aristotle determinist; it is simply logic. It defies necessity, which is not a matter of opinion. I think this is a basic component of the idea of necessity in our culture since the organon.

DAVID BYRNE: There are various tools I use. One which I've gone into quite recently is a comparative analysis technique which is based on cases or on variables although it is designed to produce varied descriptions of the cases. In there, very straightforwardly, is an idea of both necessary and sufficient causes. It is a Boolean algebra technique that uses ideas developed by electrical engineers about switching theory in the 1940's. The illustration I use to demonstrate this to my students concerns differentially successful U.K. secondary schools. In terms of the kind of quality of description, how well you are doing and who have got in, you can look through it and it will sometimes establish necessary causes. Usually it does not. It is a sort of Galilean thing about what is the cause. It seems to me Galileo makes an ontological statement that says that is always present and always happens. But you do not often get that. You do not often get necessary causes. And even if you do get necessary causes they are not often sufficient causes. You have to have other things, which is the contingency element. Very often what we get is a different sense of contingent things that will produce the outcome. For example, in the contemporary U.K., it is perfectly sufficient for a school to be high achieving for it to be a private selective school. Of course we all started out by asking the kind of big questions Immanuel Wallerstein asks—the trajectories of course, the societies, dictatorship, democracy. I am doing it at a much more problematic policy level.

KEITH BAKER: It seems to me very clear we all understood what you said, there are sufficient necessities. There are contingencies. You were in fact using the classic language of necessity and contingency. We all understood you and we have no problem with it, so I'd like to ask Immanuel [Wallerstein] what was wrong with that.

IMMANUEL WALLERSTEIN: It is a question of what language will get you closest to a description of reality. In fact what is called necessary conditions is always open to challenges. Necessary conditions is one of the premises of modern science. Indeed if we look at the history of science, these necessary conditions have constantly been overthrown. People have asserted X, Y, and Z as a necessary condition of whatever and then 50 years, 100 years, 200 years later it turned out not to be a necessary condition because we have done further work and so forth. So in point of fact we have been pursuing a will-of-the-wisp. Perhaps what we want to do is come up with the most plausible explanation that simplifies the language—the most plausible explanation that we can construct, of whatever it is that we are studying, which we know is not perfect but which makes no pretense of being a statement of what is necessary and what is contingent. It is simply plausible. It works better than any other explanation that we have at present, given the degree and the state of our empirical knowledge and our playing around over time with similar situations repetitively. We say, yes this is a plausible interpretation.

DAVID BYRNE: I think that is absolutely fine, because the kind of thing I am talking about is true in particular sets of social circumstances for a particular period of time. I think it is interesting as well, in your words, your level of necessity can be point 8 [.8] occurrence and that becomes a necessary description. But that is a tool for a certain kind of action.

IMMANUEL WALLERSTEIN: You are not using the word necessity. You are really talking probability. And that is what I said. Let us do probable versus improbable. Point 8 [.8] is more probable than point 6 [.6]. I do not disagree and I am perfectly happy to use that kind of language.

BOAVENTURA DE SOUSA SANTOS: I don't think that we solve our problems by just getting rid of necessity among the absolute antinomies. We know there is one specific feature of intermediate concepts: they admit they are imbedded in a range. Where are the outer limits of the range? We may be back to square one. And that is the trick of Kant. Nietzsche showed it very well and he gets in by the back door. So with this type of position, I would like see that we work on our particular social science intermediate, original concepts. We should design in our philosophy and social sciences ways in which this absolute concept—necessity, chance, or whatever—would be neither paralyzing nor empowering, just entertaining the human condition.

ELIZABETH (BETSY) ERMARTH: I know of nothing more challenging to the very assumptions of modern science than what I call poststructuralism. I don't just mean Derrida or his followers, or any single influence for that matter; and I certainly don't mean anything like the trivialized version of postmodernity disseminated in the U.S., but not abroad, by theorists who are unaccountably influential over here. What qualifies as poststructuralism is much bigger than you would know from U.S. sources. After a decade in the U.K., I'm impressed by how much Europeans have taken in this powerful challenge to empiricism, used what they could and jettisoned the rest, and how little we have done so over here, where we are still cycling in denial. For me, the terms poststructuralism and/or postmodernity indicate the paradigmatic shift at the end of, and away from the common denominator universe that took hold across the range of practice during the centuries between 1400 and 1900, roughly. The paradigmatic shift beyond modernity is probably equal in magnitude to the one that can be characterized as "postmedievalism"—i.e., from what we call the "Renaissance." There are various versions of this shift. Einstein, Saussure, Picasso: each of them achieved in a different medium a similar move away from objectivity and toward measurement, away from the conventional Newtonian/Enlightenment constants or common denominators of time and space. Each moved from object to measurement and from discrete entities to systems. That is why language, understood as a system, not as a series of pointers, that is, words—as Foucault and Saussure understood it—is such a powerful new model. One of the main casualties of this shift is the dualisms that support the rationalizations of modernity. I focus, for example, on modernity's production of medium-neutrality and thus of the possibility of objectification which did not exist before, at least not in any disseminated way. These values are the precondition of any empirical experiment or measurement (not to mention representation in art and politics, and so on). These values are the precondition of still-prevailing modern definitions of identity and of sequence which are increasingly inadequate to the contemporary world. These are the values radically challenged by postmodernity, and not just here and there among quirky Francophiles, but across the range of practice; and not just from wishing to shock the bourgeoisie, but from recognition that because other approaches now work better than traditional methods and models. If scientists don't get it, that may be because they have allowed themselves to coast on the prestige of technology. But science, and especially social science, isn't technology, and unresponsiveness to these challenges only harms science and does nothing to forestall the challenges which are already in place—they are not hypothetical.

HELEN LONGINO: Hearing Kant invoked I thought, "What was Kant doing?" Kant was proposing, and I will defer of course to the historians of philosophy here who will possibly correct me, that there are a priori laws of thought through which we must think the world. They constitute conditions of any possible experience.

I think of his example of the boat in the river. You cannot think of the boat in the river at position Y without thinking of it as having been earlier at position X whatever that was. It is always coming down the river from someplace. That is the kind of necessity in our very thinking that Kant was postulating. But Kant lived in a Newtonian world and he was articulating a metaphysics for a Newtonian world. I think what many people here are saying is that actually we are in a post-Newtonian world and we are in a post-Laplacian world so we need different metaphysical concepts to elaborate the understandings of that world. That is where I find some sympathy with Prof. Wallerstein's suggestion that we get rid of necessity. We have been carrying it around with us for thousands of years but maybe it is time to get rid of it and move on to some different concepts. We could probably do this. We could think of different kinds of conditions other than necessary and sufficient conditions. We can think of restricting conditions and enabling conditions, both of which carry in them probabilistic notions. Non-deterministic causal factors. Non-absolutes. Maybe it is notions like these. But of course we need to look at the more direct ways we have now of understanding the world, the sciences that were produced in various ways, as David Byrne was suggesting we do. Look at the kind of work that he is interested in and find the metaphysical notions that are going to carry across different sciences if we want metaphysical elaboration. Maybe we do not even need them. But I think we do.

DAVID BYRNE: We do.

HELEN LONGINO: We do seek them. But perhaps Western thought is at a point where it needs some different ones and it might find them in other modes of thought or it may have to invent them.

ALEXEI GRINBAUM: Well, I agree and I disagree. We can talk about causality for the world on a condition that we make this causality probabilistic causality. The notion of probability intrinsically belongs to causal chains. You cannot remove it from causal chains. Causal chains are formulated in terms of probability. There is another level where necessity comes in and that is when you are saying probability 3% or probability one. So what is 3%; what is one? There is this necessary aspect of quantization because the numbers are an element of an intersubjective agreement plan of which the fact that you introduced the language of concepts like 3% or one is a necessary thing. There is no probability on that. Otherwise we cannot communicate. So there is some room left for necessity.

HELEN LONGINO: But what is the necessity?

IMMANUEL WALLERSTEIN: What you are saying now is that all statements are quantitative. It is more or less; it is three-quarters or one-quarter. It is 79.2% versus what? Whatever we say about the world is quantitative. It is just quantitative in a very minimal way, more or less, or it is quantitative in more detailed fashion. And that is true.

HELEN LONGINO: Is the condition of possibility the mathematical representation? Is that what is a condition of possibility?

ALEXEI GRINBAUM: I would say a condition of possibility of mathematical formalization is a condition of possibility of theories but we are not only speaking about theories. But if we are saying, let us look at probabilistic causation and see if there are any necessary elements left in this theory, then I am saying the necessary element is at another level. There is a condition of possibility of probability and when you say 3%, someone else should have the same idea of 3%.

HELEN LONGINO: But that is a necessary condition for communication. That is not a necessity in the world.

ELIZABETH (BETSY) ERMARTH: I would like to reintroduce the idea of language here. It has come up in a lot of the things that have been said. By language I do not mean verbal language only. I mean the idea of language as a model for any and all mental cognitive activity. That is the idea that can be found in poststructuralist theory mostly in Leotard and Saussure, at least in my sense of Saussure. We tend to be talking here about one world. We are talking about the laws, of the not laws, of the necessities or the contingencies of a world that is one. It is one and same world and we are trying to describe it and discuss it from various viewpoints. But we are assuming that we are talking about that world. Now if you accept the language hypothesis that I think is very interesting and productive, you accept that the world does not exist. There is no THE world. There is no THE time, there is no THE past. Instead you have systems and irreducible differences. That does not strike me as a tragedy but it does make description a completely different kind of problem. It may make science impossible, but I hope not. It seems to me that it is precisely language that is, I would not call it categorical, maybe a categorical imperative. We will call it that. The thing without which you cannot have any cognitive recognitions at all, but in so doing, inhabiting a language, and I am insisting that it is not the verbal language we are talking about, but any kind of a differential system of meaningful discourse, that generates meaning and value. Politics, marriage, fashion, you no longer have a common denominator world. You simply have to identify your language. I come back to what Keith [Baker] was saying about the catastrophic situation that he imagined in which you do without antinomies and you try to figure out what you are doing with other people and what you are going to call it. And you are saying you are not going to re-invent the wheel everyday, you need necessity. I do not think so. I think you need to figure out what your language is and it gets a little messy but it is not frightening. I think we all do it normally anyway, everyday. We are constantly specifying in one way or another all kinds of things, and in a way that our intellectual model does not allow. What we need is an intellectual model that will allow us to accommodate that quite sophisticated usage that we are accustomed to anyway. But I think it rules out necessity and it rules out a common world except that everyone uses language.

JOÃO CARAÇA: I'd like to introduce here the question of power, in fact. This way of thought that we have entertained for 2500 years was based on a logic of values, the principle of excluded thirds. There was a good reason for introducing it because it allowed thinking, rational thinking as we think today. Now the problem of fuzzy logic is that it is a logic of three values. This means that there is value to what is in between. The question is, what does it mean for the human predicament to be introducing a logic of that type. We know it works. In elevators nowadays it is fuzzy logic that commands the elevator to arrive smoothly to the floor. The question is, by losing necessity we are also losing universality; we are losing all these things, omnipotence. That is the trouble, if science in fact was an emancipation from theology. And I agree. We sometimes say that there was the fight between science and religion. It is not religion; it is a fight between science and theology which was won. But it does not mean that illusion is not there. For example in the United States you don't have a religion, but you have freedom of belief. So we have several religions. People say that they have their own God but there is an institution where you have freedom of belief. Now the question is, was there a good thing about God, which was omnipotence? So we felt safe. Now somehow the nation-state filled that place. And the question is, by losing necessity we lose omnipotence, we lose universality. What are we getting back?

JOHN MARTIN FISHER: David [Byrne] said he was a tool user and that is the way he liked to think of these things. The usefulness of the tool presumably can be separated from the motivations for the individual who created the tool. The etiology of the tool is a separate issue from the usefulness of the tool, so I think we should be careful about committing something like the genetic fallacy. If we attribute to religion this tool of necessity that may be the etiology but it doesn't necessarily entail it, it is not useful. What I like to do is let a thousand flowers blossom. Let us keep a notion of absolute necessity and then also various other kinds of weaker notions of constraints and so forth. Explanation is pragmatic, value driven, and we should not expect all explanations to have the same form.

STEVE FULLER: Two points. The first one having to do with the point that Betsy [Elizabeth Ermarth] made about language. I think in a way it relates to the point that John [Martin Fisher] has just made. A lot depends on how we conceptualize language here because it seems to me you are thinking about language like natural languages existing independently of each other, or at least bounded from each other in that sense or separate. But what if one thinks about language again with an eye to an idea of a universal language? Let us say Chomsky, where all the different natural languages are some kind of particular realization of a common potential. Where certain rules are actualized and others are not actualized. Nevertheless at the end of the day you have an overarching conception of language that in practice is constrained in different ways in different settings. One can still have a validity notion, the idea of a unified conception of how all these languages relate to each other. We still have a way of bringing back this more universal, general kind of idea, at least in principle. The other point goes back to this question, which I take to be quite important to this conference, of how does all this bear on research. Dave [Byrne] has been particularly talking about this. It seems to me that worrying about whether we should be keeping necessity or favoring probability is not so important. For those of us who do empirical or historical research, how is the kind of research that we do, the kinds of findings we come up with, how do they bear on the modal character of claims? If we are trying to shift probability 1 or 2 percentage points one way or another, how exactly does that work? What is the language game within which researchers are able to make those kinds of modal moves? I think this is a more interesting question than worrying about would we want to work with some kind of robust absolute conception of necessity. We do want to work with some notion of modality. That is something we all agree on here. The question is, how does empirical research or historical research shift the modal quantifier on statements that we want to make about the relationships that govern the world? It seems to me that we should be continually returning to that.

JEAN-PIERRE DUPUY: But would you say the same of the possible as a modality?

STEVE FULLER: There is a very interesting question that is not fully resolved about how empirical research bears on modal character statements.

JEAN-PIERRE DUPUY: Precisely.

STEVE FULLER: Right, and I think it is something that needs to be discussed more because it is not too hard to come up with formal simulations and we are doing a lot of that this morning. But the exact relation to empirical research is why empirical people and historians are often skeptical about the idea of modality altogether.

JEAN-PIERRE DUPUY: Historians are writing counterfactual histories.

DAVID BYRNE: What Steve [Fuller] said is interesting because I have this kind of game which relates back to the whole business about impossible, possible, probable, thirds: it's an absurd kind of game. And it may be something many of you who teach statistics do with students to try and get them to understand the ideas about probability. Probability does seem very general and people have very poor conceptual structures about probability. It often seems counterintuitive. You know the trick question: how many people do you have to have in the room for two of them to have the same birthday? The answer is an incremental build. I think this is a good deal of what we are talking about: this kind of incrementalism, a kind of different conception, thought in terms of discretes. This is a way of building continuity that might help us. And actually that is why a great deal of probabilistic decision making is interesting.

JOHN MARTIN FISHER: Just a quick point. Maybe this is obvious, but when we say 3%, that is remarkable. It is really a purpose and context driven thing. For instance, recently we found out that one of my kids had braces when he was younger and now the dentist said we are going to have to break his jaw and reset it. It turns out that some percentage of people who have this type of dental work need to have this done. I said, What percentage? He said, 4% actually. I thought 4% was remarkably high. Four percent and he did not tell us. But you know you can imagine lots of other contexts where 4% would not seem so high. Your podiatrist makes an orthotic for you and fails to tell you that in 4% of the cases they have to adjust it a little later. You would not say that is remarkably high, even though the percentage is the same. It is a matter of what is at stake.

DETERMINISM AND MATHEMATICAL MODELING

Ivar Ekeland

I

Rien ne se perd, rien ne se crée. Nothing gets lost, nothing gets created. This is the basic law of chemistry, as formulated by Lavoisier in the late eighteenth century, precisely the time when the concept of determinism takes shape. Just a few years later, Laplace will make his famous pronouncement that if some rational mind (a demon) was farseeing enough to envision the whole universe at one glance, and agile enough to perform instantly and exactly all the calculations it wanted, then the future and the past would lie before it as an open book.

Indeed, there is a strong similarity between these two views of the universe. Determinism can be understood as Lavoisier's law applied to information. What Lavoisier is saying is that, in spite of all the apparent changes that take place in a chemical reaction, the basic constituents remain unaffected. When sodium and chlorine are put together, they disappear and an innocuous substance appears, namely salt. This is quite a spectacular experiment (not one you would want to perform on your kitchen table), but it is fundamentally an illusion. Neither the chlorine nor the sodium have disappeared, they are hidden in the salt, and they can actually be retrieved with the proper apparatus. The same atoms of chlorine and the same atoms of sodium are still present; they have just been combined in a different way.

Determinism is basically the belief that *no information is ever created or destroyed.* There can be no gain of information between today and tomorrow (so that, if you know the state of nature today, you should be able to predict the state of nature tomorrow), and there can be no loss of information between today and yesterday (so that, if you know the state of nature today, you should be able to reconstitute the state of nature yesterday). It might be difficult to retrieve that information, just as is it difficult to separate the chlorine from the sodium in ordinary salt, but it is just a matter of having the proper apparatus and being able to perform the calculations.

This is a strange idea, for it runs directly counter to our everyday experience. However, it is well-grounded in religious and philosophical thought. We can refer to the classical idea that God has a great Book, where He has written in advance everything that will happen to everyone, so that we find ourselves miraculously playing our appointed role without ever having learned it, discovering its most unpleasant parts as we go with the word *Mektoub*, "it is written." This has the advantage of putting us in the comfortable position of blaming someone else for our own failings, but Leibniz managed to twist the idea around and put the blame back on us. For while Laplace's demon sees only one universe, Leibniz's God sees infinitely many, where there are infinitely many independent copies of myself doing infinitely many different things for infinitely many different reasons. The trick is for God to bring to existence only one of these universes, thereby thrusting its inhabitants onto the stage of life. God is innocent, as in Plato. He merely gives the poisoned gift of existence to creatures who have already made their decisions, and who are condemned to enact them as they have conceived them of their own free will. The other universes that are not singled out in this way remain as possibilities in God's mind, and it seems to me that Leibniz at this point has been short of imagination. Had he stated that all these universes existed simultaneously, he would rank today as a precursor of the "multiversum" theory in contemporary physics.

Let us climb down from these lofty heights, and have a look at everyday life. We know a fair amount of what is going to happen tomorrow, but by no means everything. No one would attend a sporting event if the result were known beforehand; there would be neither spectators nor competitors. In fact, the very word "event" conveys some element of surprise, and so does the word "happening." In French, the word "non-event" (non-événement) has been coined to designate an event that is devoid of that element of surprise, something that has been long anticipated and happens precisely as expected. We expect to be surprised, and sometimes we even surprise ourselves: we act in ways we did not anticipate beforehand, and do not understand afterwards, and we call that personal freedom.

So where does the idea of determinism originate? Probably in the language, like so many things. The question "why" starts from the effect, the answer "because" points to the cause; both are present in all Indo-European languages, and I would guess in all others as well. Each of these describes a link in a causality chain which can stretch very far in both directions, a strand of determinism in the flow of events. Many of the properties we have seemingly discovered in the twentieth century, with the help of mathematical models and computing power, are already present in the language. Take chaos theory, for instance, and remember the old saying: for want of a nail, the battle was lost. Indeed, since the nail was missing, the horseshoe fell off, and then the horse stumbled, and then the king fell, and then his followers fled, and then the battle was lost. Is this not a perfect illustration of the so-called sensitivity to initial conditions? A very small cause, so small as to escape notice, eventually balloons into a major effect. We can also reverse time, and ask ourselves, what is the cause of the king's fall? Well, it is not only the missing nail, it is also the fact that the king was riding his horse into battle, and then we have to throw in all the causes that led to the battle taking place at that particular place and time, as well as all the causes that led to the nail missing from the hoof, so that eventually it will appear that the whole universe conspired against the king that day. This is another feature of chaos theory, and more generally of nonlinear models: as one goes farther back in time, the number of causes that can be attributed to a given event multiplies, so that eventually it encompasses the whole universe.

We can also claim that determinism emerged from experience. There is some measure of predictability in the world around us, and it decreases as one moves from natural to social interactions. There are rarely surprises when we throw an object:

we may not be able to predict the trajectory of a boomerang, but the trajectory of a stone can be relied upon. Dealing with people is a different matter: after the initial greetings, we will not necessarily be able to steer the conversation in the direction we expect, and it is precisely that unpredictable part that is the charm of human conversation. This is undoubtedly the reason why mathematical models of behavior first emerged in the natural sciences, before crossing over to biology and then to the social sciences. Their use has honed the concept of determinism, and we shall proceed to examine how it survives the journey.

II

Pure, true-blooded determinism expresses itself in differential equations. Arguably the greatest mathematical achievement of all times was the discovery of calculus, which is basically a tool to model continuous motions. A differential equation expresses a relation between velocity and position. This relation is supposed to hold throughout the motion, and it is sufficient to completely determine the trajectory from the initial position.

Every law of classic physics is expressed as a differential equation, the most famous of all being the law of gravitation, which states that the acceleration a is related to the distance r by ar^2 = constant, and which results in the trajectory being an ellipse, as Newton famously proved. Conversely, using a differential equation to model any phenomenon automatically implies the basic law of determinism, namely that the present state fully determines all future states, and that time can be run backwards to give all previous states as well. Laplace viewed the history of the universe as a single trajectory of a huge differential equation, so that knowing the present state would indeed determine all subsequent ones. If we try to fit the story of the missing nail into that view, we would express it as saying that a small change in the initial condition (the horse's hoof) has shifted the system from one trajectory (where the battle was won) to another (where the battle was lost). This immediately brings up the question of what we mean by "changing" the trajectory;

there is one and only trajectory, the universe is firmly set on its path since the beginning of time, when it was in fact already written in the available information that a nail would be missing many billions of years down the road. And it is indeed a paradox of determinism that it destroys the very notion of cause which it is supposed to uphold. For saying that something is the cause of something else means that the second would never have happened without the former, that is, that the world could have been different than it actually is. But in a fully deterministic world, the course of history was irrevocably set after the Big Bang, so that imagining that a certain event (the cause) could have been otherwise is counterfactual, and ultimately meaningless. Saying that if I had not shot him, Jack would still be alive, makes precisely as much sense as saying that if the bullet has changed into a flower in mid-air, Jack would still be alive. My life history is as fully determined as the trajectory of the bullet, and there is no more reason to incriminate me as a murderer than to incriminate the bullet as an accessory to crime.

There are obviously physical systems which are not deterministic, in the sense that one is unable to predict future states from the current one. This is the case, for instance, when throwing dice. Whether the system is truly unpredictable, or whether it is just an effect of scale, so that the relevant information, which would indeed help us to predict future states, is hidden away at the microscopic level, is another matter, and we have discussed it elsewhere (Ekeland 1993). To model such random systems, one now uses probability theory, the basic tools of which were developed in the nineteenth and twentieth century, right after the foundations of calculus had been firmly established in the eighteenth century. Actually the name of Laplace serves as a link between the deterministic and the probabilistic approach (Laplace 1812, 1814). He is known as an ardent proponent of determinism in science, but he is also one of the first scientists to take into account the cumulative effect of many random shocks, whereby independent fluctuations average out to a deterministic outcome. This is nothing more (but nothing less) than the belief that if one throws a fair dice a great many times, although one can never predict the outcome of a particular throw, one can predict that the average frequency of sixes will eventually become very close to 1/6.

Of course, the mathematics of probability theory, being mathematics, and hence a pure formalism, proceed without worrying about the connections of the model with reality. This is for eventual users to worry about. We now have a well-developed stochastic calculus, which combines classical calculus with probability theory, and which can be used to model random dynamical systems. The end users, physicists, engineers, biologists, and economists, now have the choice between two categories of mathematical models, the deterministic ones, based on differential equations, and the stochastic ones, based on stochastic differential equations. The first ones are to be used if the system to be modeled is believed to be deterministic, and the second ones if it is believed to be random, that is, if the present state of the system does not fully determine the future states. In the latter case, one cannot predict the evolution of the system from a given state, but one can compute the probability of each possible outcome. To connect the theoretical results with experiment, natural scientists will then understand the computed probabilities as averages to be observed over a large number of trials, whereas social scientists, who usually do not have the luxury of freely reproducing experiments, will resort to the Bayesian interpretation (more about this later).

The distinction between deterministic and stochastic models is not as clear-cut as it seems. On the one hand, it has become widely understood in later years (although it never was a secret among mathematicians) that deterministic models may outwardly behave like stochastic ones: this is the basic content of "chaos theory." This is what happens when throwing a die: once it has left the hand, its trajectory is fully deterministic, so that if we once throw a six, we could throw another simply by reproducing the same gesture. The apparent randomness is entirely due to our inability to perform the same motion twice, which reminds us of Heraclitus stating that one cannot step twice into the same river (Plato 1998). We certainly could go through a very similar motion, but not exactly the same one, and anyway the exterior conditions would have changed, as the water in the river will have between one step and the next. On the other hand, stochastic models, if you do not look at individual results but focus your attention on averages, are as reliably predictable as deterministic ones. Gases, for instance, are understood as large numbers of molecules with random velocities bouncing off each other and any obstacle they find in their path; by the magic of statistics, at the macroscopic level where human senses operate, these random motions average out to two measurable quantities only, temperature T and pressure P, which are related by the perfectly deterministic equation $PV=RT$.

So clearly one should speak of the overwhelming success of determinism in physics. One might even say that it is inbuilt in the mathematical models that are used to model natural phenomena. One should, of course, point to modern developments. General relativity, although it uses perfectly deterministic models, challenges the very notion of time that underlies our understanding of determinism. On the one hand, it states that the distinction between past and future is valid only for events that happen at the same location; it follows that certain observers might find that Jack was dead before I fired the gun, in which case I could hardly be held responsible for his death. On the other, it does away with the sharp distinction between time and space, and treats them together in a four-dimensional geometry which absorbs the three-dimensional dynamics, so that we are no longer observing trajectories in a three-dimensional world but points in a four-dimensional one. Everything is now static, as it is in the mind of Leibniz's God, who sees our entire life at a single glance, as immediately as we see a pencil lying on the table. At the other end of the scale, going from cosmology to elementary particles, one finds even more complicated situations, where space and time are just a few of many relevant variables, most of which are not accessible to our senses, but stage complicated geometries where the very idea of causality associated with determinism is hard to pin down: the world exists globally, once and for all, and what we see as an unfolding sequence of events is just a thread pulled out of an intricate fabric. This may be the very essence of determinism, but at this point it does not say much more than the classical observation of Parmenides: "What is, is, and what is not, is not."

III

Before we cross over to the social sciences, let us say a word about the fate of determinism in biology. Certainly no one in his right senses would claim that given the conditions on the primeval Earth, one would have been able to figure out the rise and fall of the dinosaurs. At that scale, the theory of evolution is not predictive, nor does it claim to be. However, it is, at a smaller scale. Darwin himself, in the opening chapter of *The Origin of Species*, takes care to point out how successful and precise selective breeding can be, so that an expert pigeon breeder could produce any desired shape of beak or color of plumage within a few generations. Dogs, cows, crops have been evolved to order, and now of course we are not even going through the breeding process, but tailoring the phenotype directly by genetic engineering. How such a deterministic system becomes so obviously unpredictable on a wider scale or at shorter range is an interesting question, but we will not go into it, because the mechanisms we will discover will appear even more clearly as we now move into the next domain.

Economics and sociology began as offshoots of physics. The temptation was great to believe that there were laws of economics and laws of sociology, as there were laws of physics, and that the aim of these new sciences was to discover them. This belief finds its most naïve expression in Auguste Comte's "law of three stages" (*la loi des trois états*), which is supposed to apply to every human society, and which is as deterministic as Newton's law of gravitation. In the twentieth century, more sophisticated approaches were developed, and the field of theoretical economics is today very formalized, but very different from theoretical physics. The same mathematical models are used, both deterministic and stochastic, but in economic theory, as opposed to physics, there are some parts of reality which are not, or cannot, be modeled. Whatever one does with it, one will never have a complete description, and so the whole issue of determinism is moot.

Let me begin with a basic description of the prevailing model in economic theory. It deals with individuals who are supposed to be rational, members of a species which is not *homo sapiens* but *homo oeconomicus*, a cousin who is deemed close enough so that his behavior should be similar to ours. Rationality is taken in the Weberian sense of *Zwecksrationalität*: it is not meant that individuals choose their objectives rationally, whatever that means, but that, given the objectives they have, they adjust their actions so as to attain them, and that they always act out of intelligence and experience rather than out of stupidity and caprice. Mathematically speaking, this translates into the well-known model whereby people have an inbuilt utility function, and always choose the action the consequences of which will give them the largest possible utility. They are also supposed to be Bayesian, meaning that they are adept at probability theory, and that they learn from experience according to certain well-defined rules. If they are uncertain about the consequences of an action, then they will apply their knowledge of probability theory to compute the expected value of the utility, and that is what they will be trying to maximize.

Note that this is, at best, an *incomplete* theory, for it does not explain how the individual picks his objectives (or, in mathematical terms, where the utility function comes from). Being incomplete, it cannot be cataloged as deterministic or not, because it does not give an account of how the objectives (the utility functions) change with time. Perhaps it is part of a larger theory, which would give such an account, and which would be deterministic or stochastic, but we certainly have no clue whether such a complete theory exists or not, and believing that it does is strictly a matter of faith. As it is, though, it has some very interesting features, which are hard to reconcile with any kind of determinism.

Classical determinism, Laplace-style, states that the present state of the universe fully determines its future history. There is a straightforward causality line, leading from today to tomorrow, in the direction of which entropy increases: this is the famous arrow of time. Not so in economic theory, for what will happen tomorrow will depend, not only on what the state of the economy (the fundamentals) is today, but on what people think will happen tomorrow (the anticipations). In other words, we could imagine some God making a copy of the planet Earth as it is at this very moment, and so exactly that no physicist would be able to tell the copy from the original. Determinism tells us that the histories of the two planets will have to be exactly the same. Imagine now God reaching into the minds of the inhabitants of the duplicate Earth, and changing their expectations, so that people who were pessimistic about the future in the original become optimistic in the copy. Economic theory (and good sense, for that matter) tells us that the histories will separate very quickly, and from then on each will go its own way. So there is a clear contradiction here, unless one is willing to accept that, by a thorough examination of the body, a physicist would be able to tell an optimist from a pessimist, a very extreme form of reductionism.

In other words, in economic theory, the closed link in the causality chain, situation today → situation tomorrow, is replaced by an open link, (situation today + anticipations about tomorrow) → situation tomorrow.

It is clearly going to be very difficult to find a way of reducing the second scheme to the first one. And yet, I would like to stress that we are at the very heart of the social sciences. What distinguishes them from physics, for instance, is the fact that human beings are endowed with consciousness, whereas atoms are not, so that humans will collect information and act upon it, whereas atoms will not. The publication of Newton's *Principia* certainly had no effect on the movement of celestial bodies; certainly neither the Sun nor the Earth cared very much about the discovery of the law of gravitation. But if some guru manages to convince enough investors that sunspots cause stock markets to fall, they eventually will, even though there is no rational foundation for such a belief, except the fact that it is shared by a great many people: the prediction becomes self-fulfilling. Indeed, if I so believe, the appearance of sunspots will serve as a warning to me that the economy is entering a downturn, and I will sell on the market, thereby driving down prices; if I am the only one to do so, it does not matter, but if there are many of us, the stock market will start dipping, thereby confirming the original belief and convincing others to join the trend.

In the social sciences, *theory shapes reality through belief*, whereas the natural sciences hold a Platonic view, whereby physical reality exists independently of the observer and cannot be influenced by the opinions he or she holds. This observation lies at the heart of the famous Lucas critique of economic forecasting. It used to be the case in developed countries that one would build models of the economy as a whole, adjust them to the current data, let them run into the future, and then announce the results as forecasts for the real economy. This is precisely how trajectories are computed in physics, but Robert Lucas pointed out such forecasts influence the very results they are supposed to predict, because they change people's expectations, except, of course, if they were kept secret, an interesting thought! This does not mean that forecasting is impossible; it just means that it has to be done in a less crude way, so that changes in expectations are accounted for, and this is the research program of the new school of econometrics, led by Jim Heckman.

Let me now go into some of the methods which have been developed to make economic theory complete, that is, to include some description of the way individuals form expectations and change them as they go. The most ancient way of modeling these changes is the Bayesian approach. It basically states that people are able to assign probabilities to events, even in cases when empirical data is not available, so that they cannot resort to the frequency interpretation, and that they change these probabilities according to certain mathematical rules when new information comes in. Bayesian theory is quite explicit about those rules, and quite vague about the way initial beliefs are formed. In games of chance, like dice or poker, which are played repeatedly, events can be assigned objective probabilities, which are their average frequency over a large number of trials. But there are many situations where decision-makers face one-time events, which never occurred before and will not be repeated, such as a sporting event, or an election. The fact that people are willing to place bets on the outcome of such events proves that they are able to assign probabilities to them. Such probabilities now vary with the individual, and the information he has, so that they are called subjective. If, for instance, I am willing to take an event bet that candidate A will lose the U.S. presidential election, but I refuse 4-to-5 odds, then my subjective probability of candidate B winning lies between 1/2 and 5/9. How subjective probabilities are formed is a subject shrouded in mystery, although, in my opinion, it lies at the heart of human decision-making.

Imagine entering a room full of one-armed bandits (not humans, but slot machines), with a bag of coins in your hand. All the bandits are different, some are old, some are new, and you are told that some of them give you better chance than others. How should you play your coins? Should you choose one machine and stick to it? Should you change machines randomly? It seems clear that you should spend some time, and some coins, trying out the machines, so as to locate the one that gives the best odds, and then stick to it till your bag is empty. But the devil is in the details: since you have only one hundred coins, you cannot afford to spend too many during the first phase, so at some point you will have to decide you have enough information to shift to the second. When will that be? Initial beliefs are crucial to the answer. If you start with a very strong hunch that the red bandit in the left corner is the best one, it will take a lot of evidence to convince you that it is not, while if your initial belief is that all bandits are about the same, you will switch much more easily. Once initial beliefs are settled (and the theory gives us no clue as to how this is done), theory takes over, and there are mathematical methods available to determine the optimal strategy, although the computations are horrendous.

Now imagine a manager starting an ordinary day of work. The mail is on the desk, there are fifty messages on the computer, and the phone is ringing. All this is information trying to get to him (or her), and the problem he faces is to allocate his very limited time between all these messages competing for his attention: he has to decide what is important and what is not, which leads are worth following up and which ones are not worth his time. He also has to remember all the other leads he is currently following, and decide when it is time to abandon some of them because they are not living up to expectations. I have held some high administrative positions, and in my experience the best approximation to this kind of job is the one-armed bandit problem as I just described it. From what I have read and heard, this is typical of management positions. Company executives, government officials, and military commanders all have to allocate their time between matters calling for their attention much in the same way as the gambler allocates his coins between the different slot machines, and with as little information to start with. The way they do it, however, has very little to do with the mathematical procedure I described: they do not worry about their initial beliefs, they somehow pluck them out of thin air, and once they have chosen to follow a lead, they adapt to the stream of incoming new information without performing the extensive calculations the theory calls for.

It seems to me that our best attempt at modeling the process whereby people in power reach decisions is very far from reality, and I do not see how the difficulties I have pointed out can be overcome any time soon. How the human mind can handle complex situations without recourse to computations is a familiar problem: nowadays we can build computers which will beat the world champion, but we are no closer to understanding the way humans play chess. But I think that the formation of beliefs (or the assigning of subjective probabilities) is a deeper and more difficult problem. The way human beings deal with information is a mystery to us, and it would be quite presumptuous to postulate that it is a deterministic process, or even that it can be formalized at all. Indeed, the earliest attempt at formalization ended in a paradox. This is the famous story of Buridan's donkey, who died of hunger because it was equally distant from two bushels of wheat. This parable is a reminder that any deterministic model of decision-making (such as directing the donkey to go to whichever source of food is closest) will end up in failure. The donkey died because it was a slave to incoming information, and did not decide to discard some of it as irrelevant: the fact that the two bushels of wheat were located precisely at the same distance was fed into the system and caused it to crash, as a computer would, but certainly not a living donkey.

IV

There have been two noble attempts to model the formation of beliefs, thereby filling the gap in the Bayesian theory: the first one is the theory of rational expectations, the second is game theory. Unfortunately, both of them rely on an equilibrium approach, which means that they deal with static situations, whereby the Bayesian approach, for all its failings, is dynamic. The result is that we have no unified model describing both the formation of initial beliefs, and subsequent Bayesian learning. Nevertheless, the equilibrium approach does throw a light on problems inaccessible to the Bayesian approach. We will be approaching determinism from another side, and meeting with new difficulties.

Let us first deal with the theory of rational expectations. Consider some social parameter θ, the value of which is of interest to many members of society: the unemployment rate for instance, or some stock index. Suppose I predict that θ will rise sharply in the coming year. If I am believed, as I probably would if I were to make the prediction in some official capacity, people would react to that prediction, and adjust their own behavior accordingly. These changes in individual behavior will add up into changes in collective behavior, which will eventually affect the value of θ. If that change results in θ decreasing, my prediction is self-defeating; it is invalidated by the very fact that it is believed. On the other hand, if that change results in θ increasing, my prediction is self-fulfilling: it holds true simply because people believe it.

The theory of rational expectations holds that *rational individuals can only harbor self-fulfilling anticipations.* If not, this would imply that the logical consequences of the anticipations I have, and that I know the others to have, would be that they will eventually be disappointed, so there is certainly no point in having them in the first place. On the other hands, anticipations which have no basis in facts can be realized by the simple fact that others share them. Imagine for instance that someone comes up with a theory that sunspots negatively affect the economy. Such a theory has no empirical or theoretical support at the present time, but let us say that its author manages to convince some people. In that case, when spots begin to appear on the sun, these individuals, fearing a downturn, will reduce their investments, sell their stocks and put their money into bonds, and generally withdraw from economic activity. By so doing, they will start a downward trend, and if there are enough of them, more will join the bandwagon, and the economy will dive. After a few repetitions, the correlation between sunspots and recessions will become, if not an economic law, at least an empirical fact.

The problem with that theory, if we look at it as a way of understanding how expectations are formed, is that it is too broad. There are many self-fulfilling anticipations out there, and which ones a given society will choose to coordinate the behavior of its members is a matter the theory does not touch. We can understand that if a financial analyst becomes influential enough, his predictions will become self-fulfilling, but why do some become that influential and not others? On a deeper level, we find coordinating beliefs deeply entrenched in the fabric of societies, and how they evolve seems to me an open question. From the limited perspective I have adopted here, there is no question that we are far from a deterministic theory, which would tell us on which coherent system of beliefs to coordinate. This detour through the theory of rational expectations is nevertheless quite useful, because it throws another spanner in the wheels of determinism, by showing that things may become true simply because people believe they are. Conversely, certain predictions could be true, provided they are not known or not believed. If one is to believe that the history of the universe is already written down in a great Book, as classical determinism would have it, then certain pages would be true provided they are not read, and others could be written in, provided we agree on them.

We finally turn to classical game theory, as it was created by John von Neumann around 1950, and developed in the subsequent fifty years. Central to the theory is the concept of equilibrium, which is another way to coordinate individual expectations into a coherent whole. In the theory of rational expectations, people worry about the future value of some parameters affecting society as a whole. In game theory, people worry directly about other people's actions—all other people! So game theory is enormously more complicated: an equilibrium is *a situation where everyone has successfully anticipated the actions of everyone else*. We then encounter the same difficulties that plagued us with rational expectations. The only case where game theory has predictive power, the case when there is a unique equilibrium, occurs very rarely. Most of the time, either there is no equilibrium at all, or there are several. If there are several, well, society is supposed to settle on one of them, and the reason why it chooses one instead of the other lies outside the theory. If there are none, then it is even worse, for the theory gives no idea what is going to happen. We are in a situation which is very similar to the situation physics was in during the sixteenth century: we have a theory of equilibrium (statics), and no theory of motion (dynamics).

There have been two major attempts to write history from the point of view of *homo oeconomicus*, that is, as the product of actions taken by rational individuals.

The first one is the *History of the Peloponnesian War*, written around 430 BCE by Thucydides, and the second is Guicciardini's *Storia d'Italia*, written between 1535 and 1540. Both narratives paint history as a succession of decisions deliberately taken by rational individuals, in light of the best information available, thereby laying down a rational path, which would by itself be susceptible of formalization and modeling, but which is ever thwarted by unexpected events, ranging from human incompetence to natural disasters. Let me recall here the opening of the Peloponnesian war (book 1, §80–85). The Corinthian envoys come to Sparta, and require the Lacedemonians and their allies to wage war against Athens, whereupon Archidamos, king of Sparta, takes the floor and explains convincingly that this is a war that cannot be won. I do not know of a more convincing argument than the one Archidamos made that day (or, rather, than Thucydides makes for him): if any prediction in the social sciences can hold some certainty, that was the one. And then two remarkable things happen, almost immediately, to turn the tide of events. The first one is that the Lacedemonians do go to war, in spite of that beautiful argument; Thucydides does not expand on why they did it, corruption being as distinct a possibility in those times as it is now. The second one happens in the second year of the war (book 2, §48–53): it is the great plague of Athens, which wipes out one-third of the population. This neatly draws the limits of determinism: people are not rational, not everything can be foreseen, and unwinnable wars are eventually won.

V

To conclude, I would like to recapitulate my main argument. I have sketched a particular view of the social sciences, whereby individuals are rational, that is, behave strategically to achieve their personal objectives, and the organization and functioning of society result from some equilibrium between individual strategies. I have shown that, if one adopts this rationalistic point of view, the transition from individual to collective behavior is a barrier to determinism. The problem of coordination seems at the present time insuperable: there are usually many ways in which a collection of rational individuals can act, even if each and every one of them remains rational throughout. Pure rationality cannot decide between them, and other factors will be instrumental in deciding which one will occur.

One could also take the Hegelian view, and see society itself, not the individual, as the actor of history; individual behavior then is merely a secondary phenomenon, the effect of social pressure on the individual. Perhaps a better case could be made for determinism in such a framework. I have not done so, for lack of familiarity with such theories, not to mention lack of belief in them.

Finally, I would like to stress that the question of determinism in the social sciences is intimately tied to the question of *control*: if the behavior of individuals and groups is fully determined by external conditions, then surely by modifying these conditions one can control behavior. Religion, education, and law enforcement are traditional means to do so. Unfortunately, with the progress of science, new means of control are being developed and put in operation. The twentieth century, which invented and used weapons of mass destruction, such as nerve gases and atomic bombs, has also distinguished itself by scientifically controlling beliefs, through professional use of the mass media of communication. Brute force, the oldest means of social control, has also greatly benefited from technological progress. We are now able to maintain a whole population of several million people in an open-air prison, behind electrified fences or a security wall, keep watch over them with drones, and kill them at pleasure from a computer screen. Even torture now becomes scientific, with doctors, psychologists, and social scientists collaborating towards breaking down the individual.

But force itself may become outmoded as a means of control, soon to be replaced by genetic engineering. The inbuilt determinism of genetics brings with it a new temptation: why should we try to control the beliefs or actions of fellow human beings, when we could directly engineer loyal subjects? This is now going beyond the scope of this chapter, but there is little doubt that this and other technologies will be very relevant to the problems raised by determinism in the social sciences.

REFERENCES

Ekeland, Ivar. 1993. *The Broken Dice, and Other Mathematical Tales of Chance*. Chicago: Chicago University Press.

Laplace, Pierre-Simon, marquis de. 1812. *Théorie analytique des probabilités*. Paris.

———. 1814. *Essai philosophique sur les probabilités*. Paris.

Plato. 1998. *Cratylus,* trans. by C. D. C. Reeve. Indianapolis: Hackett Pub. Co.

DISCUSSION

JEAN-PIERRE DUPUY: From a philosophical point of view there is nothing new under the sun here, because if you are a Kantian and come to us here a follower of Husserl you can say that the nature of man is that he has no nature. So if we decide to shape ourselves far from being the height of determinism, as you said, it is the height of complete indeterminism—radical indeterminism and that is scary. Absolutely scary. So I would like to reverse your [Ivar Ekeland's] last point.

IVAR EKELAND: Yes, I just wish to say that was what I thought. If you did not see that, I expressed myself poorly.

JOHN CASTI: I would like to make a couple of comments about the underlying logical structure of this classical field of economics that you outlined, and especially the rational expectations part, because I think that I am sure that in the world of finance, the idea that if everyone believes that the dollar is going to collapse, then everyone sells and the dollar collapses—well, yes, but. In fact there is a kind of infinite regress in that kind of argument that says if I believe that you believe that I believe that you believe and so on to a point, it has to bottom out. It cannot carry on. And I know from my own experience—I mean I have formed and sold three different companies—that in the business of looking at financial markets and making decisions about what to do and the picture that the classical view gives you is one that is, I call it trend following, that is, you will continue on that path because of some kind of essentially positive feedback. But of course the most important and interesting thing from a real life point of view is not the trend, it is when it's going to turn. And the turning point does not come from the outside; it also comes from inside the system. The empirical record is very clear on exactly when the turning point comes; it comes when everybody starts believing the same thing. That is exactly the time you have to start believing just the opposite. Because that is exactly when the system starts turning around. So this picture of, let us say, of the dollar in collapse, it is, you might call it, the greed part of the fear versus greed as far as investing. But there is no fear part in that picture. I mean, I do not argue with the indeterminate, indeterminist part of it, that the question if you had enough knowledge would you be able in fact to remove this indeterminism, does this indeterminism come from an incomplete theory, or maybe in quantum theory people might call it a hidden variable or other things of that kind, or is it an intrinsic indeterminism that cannot be removed by any amount of additional knowledge or information?

IVAR EKELAND: I am going to take this very restricted point of view, and, as far as I know, all these are static theories. I know of no dynamic theory of bubbles. But what you are talking about is really the dynamics of the bubble; I do not think we have a theory for that.

JOHN CASTI: I am sure we do not have a theory. This point about initial beliefs is very analogous even to classical physics, to say that where does the initial condition come from? Well, you can go out and measure something maybe, or you make it up, or you guess it, or if I were in sort of the practical side of this game, ask what are your beliefs? What are the initial beliefs? And you would probably say something, or I would look and see how you behave and say, this is my estimate of what your beliefs are on the basis of what I actually see; but I do not think it is so much different than the situation in classical physics.

JOHN MARTIN FISHER: I should say I do not have any ax to grind here; I do not know whether determinism is true or false. For me an important thing is that I do not think moral responsibility and free will depend on it. Let me just say, a key point for you seems to be that you cannot capture information about people's expectations about the future in terms of a state of the universe, a state description at a particular time. But I think that when you said it is very implausible, it would be a kind of reductionism, I do think that most contemporary philosophers of mind are materialists who believe that our preferences and our beliefs are in fact states of the brain or somehow are not separate from states of the brain; not all of them, I mean there are dualists and so forth, but I think you would probably think that people's preferences, as opposed to their expectations, can be somehow described at a moment. So I do not see why there should be an asymmetry between preferences and the beliefs about the future or the expectations and so I think a determinist might say: "Everything you said is true, except I think we should be able in principle to capture information about people's expectations in terms of a state of the universe description."

IVAR EKELAND: Actually, the same point struck me.

STEVE FULLER: There seem to be two issues going on here in the paper. On the one hand there is this problem of trying to figure out what people's expectations and preferences are. But at the end of the day the laws of neoclassical economics apply. So there is a sense in which there is determinism right there, right above the supply and demand law of diminishing marginal utility. You just do not know where people are on the curve. But the point is, wherever they are they are going to conform to the curve. And I think that is a very important point to keep in mind, in the sense that you might say neoclassical economics is sort of the last stand in determinism in the social sciences where it has kind of disappeared everywhere else. Now in principle, I have no objection to that, but I do think it does raise a very important question that is rooted in the way in which economics has developed historically, because of course economics comes out of political economy and just at the point where the neoclassical revolution occurs in the 1860's and 1870's, there is a question that is going on that does not involve whether one should accept, let us say, the laws of supply and demand or diminishing marginal utility; those sorts of notions are kind of accepted, but the issue is exactly what is their status. In other words, are we to think about these curves that are being drawn, these sorts of laws and these principles, as somehow a representation of reality? That if we actually knew everything about the way in which buyers and sellers operate and so forth that would actually capture it; the problem is we just do not know the initial conditions and that is what we have to figure out. Or is there some sense in which these principles are meant to be normative? So in other words, if it does not look like people conform to these principles in practice, then in a sense we need social policy to come in to make the world conform to the norms, because these principles are actually meant to be principles of rationality. So when people are operating as fully self-conscious rational agents, their behavior will conform to these models. But for various reasons, having to do with, let us say, restricted trade, they may not in fact act this way, in which case then we need social policy to redress these situations. So for example, in a case of diminishing marginal utility, say we have a millionaire, and he gets one more dollar, is it better for him to keep it than to transfer it to someone else? Well, a lot depends on what you expect is going to happen as a result of that. And you might say, well, the fact that the guy has a million dollars in the first place means that he is already doing something productive with the money that he has and so therefore another dollar is probably going to help him even more. Or you might say, no, the fact that he has a million dollars in the first place indicates that there is some sort of fundamental problem in the way in which the situation is set up and so we need to actually transfer the money from him to someone else through taxation. So in fact, what I am describing right now is the dispute between John Stuart Mill and William Stanley Jevons over how to interpret this principle of diminishing marginal utility. Jevons won the argument. So, what happened was that it was taken to be a representation of how people already operate. And if it does not look like it operates that way on the surface, that is because we have not really considered all the systemic issues. We have not quite really bounded the system in the right way. And we have to appreciate the way in which the rich guy who continues to hoard more money is in fact doing more productive things and is in fact getting greater utility from the additional dollar he receives than were it transferred to a poor person. And that is why economic science can become stuck, figuring out how that is possible. It becomes a way of mathematizing the invisible hand. While on the surface it looks like the rich guy has too much money and we ought to be transferring it to the poor guy, in fact that is only because we do not understand how economics works and we have to appreciate that in fact that the rich guy, by getting each additional dollar, is doing something productive. The point I am making here is, as long as neoclassical economics has these curves and it is still very deterministic in the way it conceptualizes things, even though it cordons off these spaces where there are all these uncertainties about what people believe and desire and so forth, there are still these fundamental principles that are deterministic. The question that remains open is whether these principles, if we accept them, are meant to be representative of economic reality once we have understood it properly. Which is, I think, the way in which we think about it now within economics. Or is it meant to be normative? In which case, then it may be that actually the way economic reality operates is not so hot and we need to do something in order to make reality conform with those economic principles. I think this is a problem that arises with all these big regulative ideal type concepts that you're concerned with here, you know, determinism, reductionism, dualism. I mean one of the things that they all have in common is the fact that it is not clear whether they are meant to be representative of how reality is or whether they are meant to be normative in the sense of we are trying to get, as it were, reality to conform to these things because we think there is something really good about them. Economics is the point where such issues have been really sharpened in a way they have not been in other disciplines of the social sciences.

IVAR EKELAND: I made no claim about reality, in a way. I took a very restricted view; I said, look at the mathematical modeling, as it is, it has nothing to do with reality. Now, as far as reality goes, economic theory has nothing to say about justice affairs, for instance.

STEVE FULLER: What about welfare economics?

IVAR EKELAND: No, because welfare economics has nothing to say about social criteria. Economic theory tells you about efficiency. It does not tell you at all about justice and social criteria. The last point would be as far as the social as mathematical modeling goes, I would say is it positive or normative, I would say it is positive.

IMMANUEL WALLERSTEIN: First of all, on the business of finding out what is in people's minds, capturing that information: actually for about 80 years, we have had a subdiscipline that tries exactly to do that, it is called public opinion polling and it is based on probability theory. It is highly sophisticated and at the level of probability theory it works fairly well. It obviously is not deterministic. John Casti raised the question of self-fulfilling prophecy and the turning points, and the statement he made was, if everybody thinks that the dollar is going to fall, when everybody thinks that, when a totality of people think that, then the clever investor moves in the other direction, which means one person does not think it. That is the first thing. The second thing is, how does the clever investor know that 100% of the other people all think that? There is no way he knows that and so there is an intrinsic uncertainty which is unconquerable. Of course, some people are cleverer than other people and are better at estimating the percentage of the world that believes a certain thing and therefore can have access to more information. But obviously no one always beats the stock market and never will be able to because there is intrinsically no way of arriving at a perfect knowledge for any individual. Now, you have also raised the question of how do you know the initial conditions. Do we make them up? In fact, of course, neoclassical economists make them up all the time. To use their favorite expression, it is called "Other things being equal." Other things being equal means somebody else has to figure out the initial conditions, not me. That is, we sociologists are supposed to figure out the initial condition for the economist, but of course, we do not. And because we do not, we say that the minute you begin to think "all other things being equal" you are into the universe, you are into all of happenings everywhere, so other things are never equal; but the economists, or at least the neoclassical economists, try to get away with the game by restricting the knowledge that they need with the other things being equal clause, but that comes back to my intrinsic uncertainty. Now, Steve Fuller raises the point and this I think is very useful, that in fact when we are dealing with neoclassical economic theory or any such theory, there is a debate as to whether that extra dollar goes one way or the other. That debate is not resolved, cannot be resolved on formal rationality. That is a debate about substantive rationality. So, what happens is, under the pretense of a theory that deals only with formal rationality, there is a latent, hidden theory of substantive rationality which they use against opponents, but not against themselves. So you know, the Bush administration, for example, accuses the Democrats of social engineering if they try to push X, but in fact they have a theory of social engineering too, which they do not admit to, but instead present as a mode of formal rationality. So the next point I want to make is that formal rationality never prevails. It is impossible, it has a meaning, if you have X objective, what is the most important thing to do to get there? But in fact, we cannot live in the world of formal rationality because every decision we ever make involves what Weber called substantive rationality, and formal rationality of course is deterministic. It is the great tool of determinism and it is one further argument as to why determinism intrinsically cannot exist. I want to make one last point and that is on the business of God and humans. When we talk of a deterministic circle, we are in fact invoking a theological concept. We are in fact just simply saying that humans can substitute themselves for our image of God. It is a theological concept.

IVAR EKELAND: Which is not that in itself.

IMMANUEL WALLERSTEIN: There are two ways of using God as a social concept. We can use the concept of God to say that God is omnipotent, can do anything, right, or we can say, because God is omnipotent and can do anything, humans are constrained in what they can do. We can use it as a constraint, or we can use it as a permissiveness. Now the term of determinism precisely uses it as permissiveness and that is in fact the source of the dilemmas of the human condition. That is why I said we have to get determinism out of our language in order to use God as a constraint.

JEAN-PIERRE DUPUY: You [John Casti and Immanuel Wallerstein] said when everyone believes that the dollar is going to fall then one should go the other way; that reminded me of the practice in ancient Israel: when all the judges believed the defendant to be guilty, then they would release him or her immediately because unanimity is suspect, I mean, it means that—

IMMANUEL WALLERSTEIN: It raises suspicion.

JEAN-PIERRE DUPUY: Yes, exactly.

IMMANUEL WALLERSTEIN: That is a great system [laughter]. We should all adopt it.

JEAN-PIERRE DUPUY: Uncertainty, unanimity is always suspect in human affairs.

IMMANUEL WALLERSTEIN: I agree.

JEAN-PIERRE DUPUY: And regarding your point, Immanuel [Wallerstein], I fully concur with your radical refusal of the kind of division of labor that economists proposed to the other social scientists. Once again I am kind of reluctant regarding economic theory being the paradigm of determinism, even before the economists discovered the fundamental role of expectations as you explain very well. One could have said and some people said, actually, that the general equilibrium model was a paradigm of radical indeterminacy except in one case, but a case which has no substance, a case in which there is an equilibrium and it is unique. But if that is not the case, then what is the theory of equilibrium, it is a theory of large-scale, across-the-board coordination. Suppose there is not one unique equilibrium, then the whole problem of coordination is still there and which equilibrium people will choose and how they will manage to choose the same one—that is to coordinate. It is a model; general equilibrium is a model of radical indeterminism, not determinism. Even without or before introducing [this model] which compounds the difficulty, first the inversion of expectation about the future—

IVAR EKELAND: Yes, I agree about that. Rational expectations are a source of indeterminism.

IMMANUEL WALLERSTEIN: I had made a note when I read your text. You in effect said, he called it determinism; it is actually radical indeterminism. I am wondering whether they are not always the same thing. In his [Ivar Ekeland's] illustration of chaos theory he said "for want of a nail the battle was lost blah, blah, blah, etcetera," and he says "eventually it will appear that the whole universe conspired against the king that day. This is another feature of chaos and more generally of nonlinear models, as one goes further back in time the number of causes that can be attributed to a given event multiply so that eventually it encompasses the whole universe. Therefore its sensitivity to initial conditions is in a sense radical indeterminism." You could say exactly the same thing about a determinist theory. All determinist theories push you back and back and back and back until you encompass the entire universe. So the description that is being used to describe radical indeterminism is the description that fits perfectly for radical determinism. Well, that should not worry us that we have a term, these two terms that are supposed to be exactly the opposite of each other and the concrete description of how it works turns out to be identical.

IVAR EKELAND: I hope there is no misunderstanding. I am not saying that economic theory is deterministic.

DAVID BYRNE: A hell of a long time ago I used to solve differential equations; in an engineering mode, engineers really regard differential equations describing physical systems not as models of the universe but as information compression. It is a quick way to get something done and the particular things I used to solve, this is purely as a school student, the equations we had to solve were of the type how do you set the initial conditions so you could drop an artillery shell down somebody's chimney. The point was that although it is a dynamic system, what you are trying to do is predict an event. If you set the conditions in a particular way, you get that event. And I think that is quite an important aspect. Now that is a lot of what we do. We try to specify events, what will happen; the power of determinism is the basis for prediction. This was the stimulus from your paper where you are describing Bayesian methods. The kind of context in which I find Bayesian methods now being used regularly is in risk assessment. One example, and I have to say I think this is a militantly cynical use and purely for defense in relation to potential legal action, it is used in terms of releasing people from what in the U.K. are called secure units, that is, for people who have been imprisoned but are found unfit to plead because of mental illness, who have been guilty of extremely violent crimes, usually murder or arson. So you bring in a Bayesian method to assess degrees of probability, the risk, that if you let this particular individual go, they will uniquely and specifically do it again. As I say, it's basically so somebody can stand up in court when it happens, and say, well you know we did everything we could to assess the risk. But it is an example of what is actually a big industry, of risk assessment, an applied industry of risk assessment. And what people are constantly trying to do is use determinism, or social engineering, or whatever, to predict a specific and discrete event, but it is not a description of the universe or the social world or anything else.

JOÃO CARAÇA: I don't know if mathematical model in economics was as strong as this statement. Can I say my argument is the following: differential equations were invented to study the problem of motion, motion in nature? And in fact the scientific approach has been since then always trying to understand change. But an instrument that was devised for the study of motion which is continuous, but now we know that they are not all continuous, was subsequently applied to other domains. In chemistry, we know that motion in chemistry is reactions and so on. When you get to biology it is more complicated. What is motion in biology? Well, fortunately we have adaptations, have revolutions, but it is not the same type of motion. And when we get to economics, what is motion in economics? So by using the same instruments, differential equations, maybe we are not getting the most adequate instruments to study economic change. Maybe some new mathematics or some other mathematics has to be used in order to tackle the problem of economics. I would like to come back to the question of information being constant and change the creation of information. Determinism is in fact the capacity of having a closed description. So that is why God comes in because He knows everything.

IVAR EKELAND: OK, possibly we need another tool; unfortunately that is all we have.

RICHARD E. LEE: We have been discussing mathematics and the physical sciences that bear directly on the primary issue here. David [Byrne] was talking about, actually all sorts of people have been talking about, differential equations—very, very dangerous for those of us who are not mathematicians or from the natural sciences to venture into these deep waters. But I seem to remember from back 45 years or so ago when I was thinking about differential equations, that there were differential equations and differential equations: some completely integrable, that describe a very small subset of systems, and the most of which describing systems not having all terms completely integrable. And you can correct me on that if my wording of this is not quite right, and therefore the event that you were talking about in the case of those kinds of systems was based on at least some kind of approximation of some of the terms. And you talked about that in terms of something I think that we should be discussing, which is predictability. There is a relationship between determinism and predictability. One way of thinking about determinism is that the future comes out of the past. But that does not necessarily mean that, knowing the past as a set of initial conditions, one can predict what that future will be. And this is a development that Ivar [Ekeland] has written extensively on, coming out of science and mathematics, it is not something that social scientists, or the humanists have invented but something that scientists and mathematicians have begun to be saying recently or at least fairly loudly over the past 20 or 30 years. Another thing that we have not mentioned is that not all systems that are relevant to this discussion are describable in terms of differential equations. Many are describable in terms of difference equations. This is a whole class or set of iterative systems that are also important to the ways that we have begun thinking about determinism. It involves thinking in terms of rule-governed systems versus law-governed systems, where each single iteration is governed by a rule. But that brings up another thing. The other thing that seems to be relevant that we have not talked about here is choice. If there are systems that are not predictable, especially, if there are systems that are not predictable and that can take different directions in their evolution, then choice and creativity are elements of that future as well.

V. BETTY SMOCOVITIS: A point I want to make is to Aviv [Bergman] and to Immanuel [Wallerstein], regarding your concern that we eliminate terms like "necessity" and "determinism." I wonder if that is perhaps not dangerous, because I see the concerns associated with necessity, perhaps not again explicitly articulated by a lot of younger people, and deterministic thinking especially in the biological sciences. You ask them a question about behavior and they will respond to the nature and nurture debate and you will see classic determinism. They may not have the technical language that we have but I do think the practitioner and the younger practitioner have to engage in this conversation. They have to continue this conversation. They have got to work through these problems. Because they have got to know what they are doing and what they are thinking.

IMMANUEL WALLERSTEIN: You mean you want them to get it out of their mind?

V. BETTY SMOCOVITIS: No, I do not want them to get it out of their mind; I want them to articulate what it is that they are doing. I want them to discuss what they are doing. I think yesterday as I was listening to you, I was getting a little bit worried. It is not that I disagree with, "Oh, I wish I could get rid of some of this language," I have also thought about it at great length. I am not that far removed from where you are. But I wonder about this pragmatically, in terms of a practice, in terms of teaching, in terms of connecting to the public, because the danger here is that we sound like knowledge-making elites, rather removed from these other people who are not in this room, not inside of elite academies. We can talk to ourselves, but ultimately we have got to connect back out to whoever the public becomes. I think about it in terms of my teaching and how would I translate this into teaching younger people and I cannot eliminate this language. In fact I try to introduce them to it, to sensitize them to what it is they do as practitioners, new practitioners in the sciences.

RICHARD E. LEE: This sounds like strategic determinism as analogous to strategic essentialism. That we need it and can deploy it in a certain way, we understand what it is, we know it does not exist, but it is useful because it works in a certain way.

V. BETTY SMOCOVITIS: It exists when there are enough people out there who think it exists and it is real. All you have to do is cross from here to the evolutionary psychologists who are really strong on this campus [Stanford].

IMMANUEL WALLERSTEIN: You are giving us the Thomas theorem. Men define a situation as real, it is real and its consequences, and that is absolutely true.

DAVID BYRNE: There is one thing I want to pick up that I think relates to the idea of a small *d* determine. Yes? And look, let us think about this word "determine." One person who did was Raymond Williams, where he is looking at two sets of propositions: base determines superstructure and social being determines consciousness. He is having an argument with all three of the terms, especially in the first set of propositions. And of course there was a very mechanistic Marxism which is down to Engels and Anti-Duhring, which very much worked in the kind of big D determinism, like the solution to the differential equation. If a base is like this, then a superstructure will be like that. Williams I think said something very interesting which I think has been implicit in our discussion. He said that there is another perfectly good English meaning of the word "determine" which is not exact specification, but setting of the limits, of the boundaries of possibility. And I think that is actually what I would pick up as a small d determine, that there is something about that kind of notion of determination which is useful to us across a broad range of contexts.

RICHARD E. LEE: E. P. Thompson, along with Raymond Williams, made this point for 20 years, and found it hard to be heard.

BOAVENTURA DE SOUSA SANTOS: I am left with an uncomfortable feeling, that economics as described by Ivar [Ekeland] is neither physics nor social science.

IMMANUEL WALLERSTEIN: You are right.

BOAVENTURA DE SOUSA SANTOS: Out of those two powerful critiques of this model of neoclassical economics, one by Steve Fuller and one other by Immanuel Wallerstein, it is very clear that economics is probably the least well-equipped social science to account for human action. I mean, it is static, does not account for initial conditions, cannot say anything about preferences, is related at this point just to efficiency, nothing about social justice. Under these conditions, my question, which as I said is a sociological knowledge question, is: Why has it become so powerful? There is something wrong. Probably not with this knowledge, or the knowledge-making elites, but with the society in which we live. I think that our discussion should be bounded by this very irrational kind of result that we get from the supposedly very rational, probably the most rational, as they sometimes claim to be, in economics.

IVAR EKELAND: Well, number one, again, may I remind you of the topic of the talk, the topic of the paper: The path of determinism in mathematical modeling. So when I talk about economics, I really mean mathematical modeling in economics. So I am not trying to speak for the whole economic profession, there are other sides of economics, Marxist economics, and so on, so I am not trying to give you a full picture of what economics actually is. So it is a small part of it. But, I think it is valid in its domain. So, for instance, I happen to think that this kind of small picture is extremely valid in certain precise circumstances. If for instance you want to know how people behave towards buying insurance, if you want to know how people buy consumer goods, it is a bit like magic. If it is a very good circumstance, then you get a very good approximation. That is quite true. But as far as, for instance, why you have inflation, what would the tax system be, what your health system is going to be, then it does not provide answers. It does not give you what you are aiming for. And I think we have here, and I agree that here you had, a kind of big swindle, in the sense that economics does not tell you what to do; but it will tell you what to do if you want to meet a certain objective, and the objective is outside. But why is it so successful? That is one answer; it is very good and very efficient, in a very restricted domain. Another reason would be there is a vested interest in having it so; you have a career in social science, perfectly true. And number two, they come with very strong arguments, I can tell you, if you talk with Gary Becker or Bob Lucas, you have to have very, very strong arguments. These are strong people. So perhaps, we are not up to the typical challenge.

JOHN CASTI: Actually, what I am going to say is related a bit more to what Richard [Lee] said a few minutes ago. I just wanted to sharpen up a little bit something that Richard [Lee] said, but I also wanted to address this issue of why it is that we have such a belief in what economists tell us about the outside world when in fact, it bears almost no resemblance to what we actually see. If you could look at the actual main line academic economics and look at the kinds of predictions the economists make about what's going to happen over the next quarter, or the next year, and so on, it is almost a joke. They are so far away from what actually happens that you could have done as well by flipping a coin in most cases as listening to a consensus view of what the economists actually tell you is likely or unlikely to happen. So the self-fulfilling prophecy part of it is almost a self-unfulfilling prophecy, as things turn out, and there are probably a lot of reasons for that. But relating more back to what Richard [Lee] said and the issue of determinism: first of all, I would prefer to generalize this notion; we talk about differential equations, and a more modern term would be dynamical systems rather than differential equations. For those of you who do not have any familiarity with this it is a very simple concept; there is some space of states and those states may be points in a space or they may be a probability distribution or whatever, and there is a rule that tells you, if you are here now, then next time we will go to this place. So, a lot of dynamical system theory is about what happens in the long run. We start at this place and let time move on to infinity, and the only distinction between the discrete and the continuous in this domain is the kinds of places you might end up. But roughly speaking, it is a technical one, and it does not matter very much. There are really only two possible long-term places you can end up: Periodical, or you just keep going round and around in the same place including an equilibrium point; or, a so-called strange attractor—a ball of spaghetti, if you like, where almost every strand is unstable, and so if you push away from it, it will go off into some completely other region. But in both cases, it is completely deterministic; the uncertainty comes from the precision with which you can measure the initial state where you actually start. But, once you decided where you are starting, thereafter the rule just tells you where to go. Now, this is an almost naïve, very classical view of the deterministic process; the starting point tells you where you will end up, if you follow this rule. Now, what is more interesting and much more difficult and we have not talked about it at all, in this discussion, is the notion of the inverse problem. Saying, I want to end up here, I am starting here. What are the rules that might get me from where I am now to where I will end up? What possible rules? And in this case, in general, the answer is: There are an infinite number of rules. An infinite number of possibilities. All of which will take you to where you want to go. It does not mean anything will work, but in order to thin down how to get from here to there, you have to feed more information into the process. To shrink down the space of possibilities. Now I myself think about even what Ivar [Ekeland] said in his talk about determinism, as maybe a kind of Platonic ideal, that only exists really in some realm out beyond space and time and it does not really have anything to do with this actual world that we live in. But as Keith [Baker] pointed out there may be situations in which determinism, or some approximation of this platonic ideal is exactly what you need, and is exactly what is appropriate for the situation or whatever it is that you are trying to answer. I mean mathematical modeling is about creating a picture of a world to answer certain kinds of questions. And it is designed to answer certain kinds of questions and not other kinds of questions. They break after a certain point. And it may well be that in any modeling exercise it certainly is a case you have to throw away aspects of the real world. You have to throw away things that you know are part of the real world that you think are irrelevant to answering a question that this model is designed to address. And by the throwing away process, maybe in some cases, you can get away with saying, I'll throw away the indeterminism and I will have a process, I will deal with a process that actually is deterministic in a small d sense. It is not maybe the ultimate platonic kind of determinism, but it works for the purposes of what you are trying to do.

AVIV BERGMAN: I disagree with you when we are trying to reduce the model to its essentials. We are not trying to get rid of what would make it indeterminate but we are trying to get rid of what would make it random noise, what would make it something that is irrelevant.

JOHN CASTI: A consequence of what you throw away may be that you get rid of the indeterminacy.

AVIV BERGMAN: Maybe.

JOHN CASTI: It is accidental, it is not the objective.

AVIV BERGMAN: Yes, but let me take your example of dynamical systems. Another way of looking at strange attractors is to construct it as the probability of being in each one of those states. This is yet another description of what a strange attractor is.

ELIZABETH (BETSY) ERMARTH: Yes, well, I want to go back to something Richard [Lee] said about iterative systems and there being systems rule-based and law-based. It seems to me that we are almost entirely going to the rule-based system but that seems to me really where your paper points us. In fact I was going to congratulate you [Ivar Ekeland] and say how much I enjoyed reading this Socratic discussion, which draws a line in the sand and says, here I stop and by the way, there is this whole world of belief in value on the other side, which is required if you are going to think about not necessarily control but comprehension. I am not sure you would be happy with it, I mean, listening to the discussion, I am not sure that would be a compliment, but that is what I liked about the paper. You say at one point that you have a theory of equilibrium but no theory of motion and I am thinking in human terms motion that is a term that applies to matter but if we could apply that in human terms, could we call it action or practice?

IVAR EKELAND: Yes.

ELIZABETH (BETSY) ERMARTH: Would that be a substitute which would involve belief in value and matter? I think there are models that are rule-based. That is a theory of action or practice, or that are theories of action and practice, that language-based in particular are the ones that seem to be the most powerful. And you [Ivar Ekeland] say at one point that this would rescue you from having to say at one point as you do that we just pluck out of thin air initial beliefs. I do not think we pluck them out of thin air, I think they are, I use the word constructed. But they are even worse than that. We inhabit them and make systems within systems within systems of constructed beliefs and values that require us to do certain things. And I was talking yesterday about language, as my idea is not a tool that you pick up and put down, you are its tool. It speaks you. To paraphrase Derrida's horrible phrase that everybody objects to, the tools can be radioactive. I mean, the Judeo-Christian dialectic, for example, which calls us to freedom. And so there are ways of thinking about modeling even that are language-based, rule-based iterative systems that seem to me pretty much neglected here and absolutely necessary, if you are going to talk about human, that vital complement which you are, I think, leaving a part of determinism. But not that there is not regularity; there is rule and regularity. Did you say at one point that things that are true, that we function according to things that are true provided that we do not know them?

IVAR EKELAND: At some point I raise the possibility, yes.

ELIZABETH (BETSY) ERMARTH: Let us speak about an event for a minute. An event took place here. The phone rang in the room. Well, it was a simultaneous event, all of us were here including the phone, but our system instantly factored that out, because it is trivial or secondary or marginal. But there would be a system in which that would not be. A surprise would be a very important, or a chance thing like that would be an important thing to be included or incorporated in the description. So I am concerned that we are leaving aside our own method and not really doing the hardest thing of all, which is to step back from that saying that is true provided that we do not know it and to name it and know it, so that we can use it as a heuristic device, and determinism is a heuristic device entirely for things, determinism as an objective property of the universe. So, it seems to me that this rule-based approach is really necessary.

AVIV BERGMAN: So, let me ask you, where would you pick those rules from? It evolves, it is like God, in a sense, you know, picking those rules out of thin air.

ELIZABETH (BETSY) ERMARTH: I think we have a thousand million Ph.D. dissertations to write on describing the rule systems that we take for granted.

AVIV BERGMAN: I agree, I agree with you.

ELIZABETH (BETSY) ERMARTH: I mean, I would like to have a language, a *langue*, a set of rules for multinational corporate life, a café bar, you name it, it is open season. Because if you regard all of these as functioning systems which speak to us to an extent that we do not acknowledge, then the description is up to you, I mean, there is not a streak of creativity, as long as it provides rules that are finite and a possibility of infinite expression, in those rules, like the language, then you do not need to name the rules, really. I think methodological self-awareness is a very difficult thing to do and if we are happy in our disciplines it is something we are never called upon to do, unless we happen to find a student who pushes us that way.

IVAR EKELAND: You [Elizabeth Ermarth] caught what I was saying quite well. Socratic, I take the point. Now indeed you are at the threshold, and the question is where all these beliefs and preferences come from. It is tempting. It kind of boggles the mind because you could say these are manufactured or you are educated into that. You can say someone does it for you. Education for that and so on, your parents, the schools and so on, but then that sends you back into the preferences of the other guys who manufacture these so you are starting a recurrence. You could say it is the culture, you are born into that, but then you are set back. The boundaries of economics can be shown very clearly; for instance, do you eat dogs in this country? In this country, dogs are not in the meat market. In China, they are. Why? And you are going into anthropology. Here is the value of anthropology: you do not eat dogs, because you name them. You do not eat anything else you name. Yes, that is true, you make the connections, and these are pets. So how is culture formed and so on? And then the next question that you mention and that I find myself is most interesting is *ça parle*, We are nothing. We are just a kind of language, tools.

JEAN-PIERRE DUPUY: It speaks, *ça parle*

IVAR EKELAND: *Ça parle.* How can we think that thing?

ELIZABETH (BETSY) ERMARTH: Maybe we do not, quite. Maybe it does boggle the mind and that is OK.

JEAN-PIERRE DUPUY: It was not Derrida originally, it was Lacan.

ELIZABETH (BETSY) ERMARTH: Yes, Lacan, I am sorry. Still objectionable, but never mind. Yes, but the other thing about language as a model, that I really liked, is that it is infinitely multipliable. We are sitting here talking a language. It is English, but there is also a philosophical language and a disciplinary language and some of us are better at it than others. I am splashing around in this now without being a scientist or a social scientist. There is gender language, there is geographic language, there is all kinds of stuff going on, and it is not going on seriatim, it is going on simultaneously. So, that it is not entangled, exactly, but whether it is separable or not may be an irrelevant question. Maybe what we need to do is accept that as a premise rather than some kind of clarity and then see what we can do with it.

STEVE FULLER: First going back to the point that Boa [Boaventura de Sousa Santos] was raising about why economics is so powerful, it has to do with the physics business, it seems to me. We have got a science, especially in this sort of neoclassical form where you are trying to explain the most by the fewest number of principles. At a metascientific level, that has always been seen as a very desirable characteristic of science, which Newtonian mechanics exemplifies. And neoclassical economics, you know, is quite obvious in trying to emulate that. But also at the level of the way in which the economy is modeled, the general equilibrium model, that also is from physics. So even at that level, the shape of the modeling looks very similar. So there is a lot of trading on the reputation of physics.

Moreover, there is no competitor Social Science for this kind of role. Most of the social sciences over the years have evacuated this space and have not desired to come up with a theory, maximally explanatory under the minimal number of principles kind of approach to things, so economics has the field left to it. And insofar as that model still captures the public and the scientific imagination, being what science ought to be about, it is going to have power. And of course, because it is operating in a kind of social space, even when it does not actually capture the phenomenon it is supposed to be capturing, it can train on the normative descriptive distinction in a very opportunistic way. So it can sometimes blame the people who are not conforming to the model and sometimes it can do a few end cycles on the model depending on what is going on. And it seems to me that is what the story looks like and in a sense what it raises very clearly is the fact that this kind of model still has a lot of grip on the imagination, generally speaking. And so there are two questions. Does one want to continue this kind of way of modeling social phenomena, you know, something physics-like as it were, in terms of a closed system under minimal number of principles, or if one wants to go away from that, what does it look like? And how does one make it publicly persuasive? And this then raises, goes to the point that I originally wanted to make concerning the discussion between Richard [Lee] and Betty [V. Betty Smocovitis]. And this having to do with the force of determined determinism here. It seems to me it is more than the strategic essentials point and I think there is an issue of levels here. When people talk about strategic essentialism, they usually mean that we have to presuppose essentialism for heuristic or instrumental reasons in order to launch something, not because we really believe that there are essences, but we have to somehow presuppose it. A kind of weakened Kantian transcendental condition, maybe, or something like that. But I think that what Betty [V. Betty Smocovitis] is talking about is something a little different; it is not that one has to presuppose it, but there is a sense in which at a second order level, this is a kind of what one might call in retrospect, a *topos*. It is a kind of general form of argument and thinking about things that actually brings in a lot of stuff and in particular brings in the interface between science and the rest of society. And this is a function of a lot of these metaphysical terms across the disciplines because determinism is not just about how you organize research in a particular science. In fact, as Immanuel [Wallerstein] has been pointing out, it might not even be its primary function. In a sense it is how the sciences establish a connection with the rest of society. And that is why you see this language in determinism, the same thing applies to dualism and reductionism and to all these other metaphysical ideas. Their primary discursive function is at the interface between the public and science—where the science becomes public, where it is shown to have some kind of relevance—and this becomes very important in a teaching context, because the students are justifying to themselves as to why they are in this business, why they engaged in all this specialized research? Very few people are in it just for the problem solving, you know, for just the puzzle solving and the minutiae of it. They are in it because they think there is some larger, science-directed, social project going on. And determinism definitely addresses that in terms of the imagination of people. So, these terms, while they might not be the best terms in the world to talk about the world descriptively and so forth, they are serving multiple functions at once, they are very important interface functions, and they are kind of very much diagnostic terms of talking about how science stands in relation to society. Science can legitimate itself socially by saying hey, look, we are coming up with laws, we are coming up with these sorts of general principals, that have this kind of force. Certainly that is the way the popular literature about science goes. But once you strip that away, then what is the point of doing all this science? I mean, is it just solving these little puzzles from which we are just looking for theories that are empirically adequate for the phenomena they purport to describe? Is that the end of the story? If that is the end of the story, it is going to be pretty hard to justify science at the large-scale social level that we're presupposing in this conference. So there is a lot at stake here in getting rid of this language of determinism. Whether determinism is true is the least of our problems. But rather what is the function it serves, right, the discursive function it serves in many different sorts of registers is the most important and maybe the empirical register may be the least important one.

V. BETTY SMOCOVITIS: That is what I was saying, really, to Betsy [Elizabeth Ermarth] here, but you know in a linguistic system you talk about function, you do not talk—what is this function, you don't talk about the objective description.

JEAN-PIERRE DUPUY: I will try to defend the view that determinism is a very important concept but that determinism is not true or false, period. That it is true or false in a given metaphysics. Let me put it almost as a caricature: true is that which reinforces social cohesion and false is that which threatens to disrupt social cohesion.

STEVE FULLER: It is the exact opposite, that is what is true.

JEAN-PIERRE DUPUY: So, let me take an example. Imagine a community; everyone believes that this particular man is a traitor to the country, and the social cohesion is OK with that accusation. And then the famous writer stands up and says, "I accuse. This man is innocent." He is put in jail and dies there. Well, I do not know what John Dewey, who was living at the time, said about the Dreyfus affair to which I am referring here. Saying that this man is innocent was absolutely disruptive to French society. But had I lived at the time, I hope that I would have had the courage to stand up and say, "No, this is false. The truth is what it is." So when it comes to ethics, at times it is good to be a naïve realist. In most trials, the goal was to have the defendant himself concur with the idea that he was guilty. I mean of course, that is the maximum; it is a great art to achieve that. But, Dreyfus was not guilty; Dreyfus always maintained that he was innocent.

JOÃO CARAÇA: I was thinking that social cohesion is always obtained at the cost of something and that something sometimes is the victim.

JEAN-PIERRE DUPUY: Yes, of course. Most of the time it is at the cost to the victim.

ELIZABETH (BETSY) ERMARTH: The consensus is a terrorist apparatus. Is that what you are saying?

IMMANUEL WALLERSTEIN: He was not saying that, he was saying the opposite of that, I think. I would like to get back to Boa's [Boaventura de Sousa Santos] question about why economics is so powerful. He really knows the answer, it was a rhetorical question. Steve Fuller only gave half the answer. The half of the answer is that they are trading on the prestige of physics, and then we have to ask why physics has this prestige and so forth. But that is all true, they have been, but that is only true since Marshall. We go back to Adam Smith, Malthus, Ricardo; they were not trading on physics, there was no resemblance to physics in anything they were saying, and yet, they were powerful then. Perhaps not as powerful as now, but they were powerful then, they were listened to, they testified before these special commissions of parliament, they affected policy in enormous ways. We will get into the history of early-nineteenth century Britain in this discussion, but absolutely they were powerful. And they were powerful because they were speaking to important social policy questions on which they had answers that in fact concorded with other powerful people. It was an ideological function. Economics was powerful because it could give a pseudoscientific explanation of what people, some people, powerful people wanted to hear. And that has been true to this day. So economics is really powerful, among other reasons, partly because it trades on the prestige of physics, I agree, and trades on the prestige of a physics that is outdated; and it is the last to give way, it is the real last defender of Newtonian dynamics. They are trading on that because the general public is not aware that Newtonian dynamics is outdated and physicists do not believe it and nobody else believes it except the economists. But let me give you two stories of economists. One: twenty years ago, I was invited to a conference by Ilya Prigogine that took place in Austin, and I forget how he defined it, it was about linearity and so forth and the conference had a peculiar structure. It was a very large conference, in terms of the actual participants, and one from about every discipline. You name it, from literary criticism to mathematics, to engineering, to everything. And the conference was run simply by each one of these people speaking successively and then answering questions from the floor. I was sitting there, I was the sociologist, and I was sitting there listening to chemists, and I was listening to industrial engineers and I was listening to mathematicians and I understood every single talk. They really tried to make it clear, and I understood their point and they were all sort of on the same wavelength or otherwise they wouldn't have been invited. The last speaker was the economist. And he got up and he said, well, you know economists are not usually thought of as being into nonlinearity, but I am really into it. And he said, I go to the blackboard and I start writing. And from then on, he spoke for about ten minutes. I did not understand a word. He was the only speaker I did not understand a word that he said. Furthermore he was the only speaker in three days of conference that got not a single question from the floor. I deduced from that that nobody else understood what he said [laughter]. That's my story number one. My story number two about economists: a friend of mine, a European social democrat, who was active in politics, who was an economist by training, desired at sort of a mid-point in life to give up politics and go back to the university as a professor of economics. And, a social democrat, he went into a school of business administration. I said, you know, why did you go into a school of business administration with your values and so forth? He said, look, it is very simple, those students in the business administration, they are interested in the real world, I can communicate with them. I get the economics students in the regular department and they are not interested in the real world, they are just interested in these models. So I cannot communicate with them. And so these are my two stories of economists. I do not think economics is going to survive as a discpline, the transformations in the real world are coming, I make the prediction, I've made the prediction a number of times, that the economists as a profession are like the Soviet Union, everybody said they are pro or con, it was a very strong system and bingo, one day it just sort of collapsed. I make my prediction again, one day soon, just suddenly it will collapse, because it is so far from the real world, in practice.

IVAR EKELAND: Well, I place the opposite bet.

BOAVENTURA DE SOUSA SANTOS: It is the third half-question that is missing. I thought that you were mentioning the symbiotic relationship between this type of economics and capitalism.

IMMANUEL WALLERSTEIN: Well, of course, that is what its ideological function is, it justifies a lot, it justifies it in gross, and it justifies it in detail. Both. And people go into it, students go into it partly because they believe the ideology, partly because you can make more money doing it, both as professors, and as nonprofessors, than becoming a sociologist or a historian or an anthropologist. So there are a lot of reasons why you get students going into it and the students who go into it are predetermined. They go into it because they already believe more or less what is being preached. Look, the point is, I think all the social sciences are ideological, but this plays a more powerful function in terms of the existing society and therefore, it becomes more powerful. As well as trading on the prestige of an outdated version of physics which—so the two things work very powerfully, especially in the United States, but not only in the United States.

HELEN LONGINO: The riskiness in science is the moral riskiness which has to do with the consequences of the interventions that we might make in the world; it is of several kinds, it seems to me. There is the moral riskiness of particular interventions that we might make. Whether we are right, whether they are the appropriate interventions to make, or whether we were wrong, as we are most likely to be, can then have consequences that we cannot even predict. So there are two kinds of risk involved; then there is a third which goes back to some of the things people were saying about expectation and it is, I think, one of the things I took you to be worried about, Betty [V. Betty Smocovitis], in the pedagogical dimension of this, which is that if enough of us believe that say, genetics is capable of providing information that facilitates interventive engineering, we will adopt that way of thinking about ourselves in the world. We will confirm it by our expectations.

JEAN-PIERRE DUPUY: Yes, that was our self-fulfilling representations as well.

AVIV BERGMAN: Except that there are two parts to evolutionary biology. One which is the short-term evolutionary biology which most people think about and the other which is the long-term evolutionary biology which people don't count as part of the game. And when we are talking about the long-term evolutionary biology, we have to take into account certain elements that are outside biology, outside engineering, outside what we are capable of, that fall into the emergent property that limits what is possible. Limits what is a viable path to take, and this is something we have ability to perform.

HELEN LONGINO: That is what we do not know.

AVIV BERGMAN: That is something we have very little control over, we do not know how it will be shaped, but what I am saying is that if we were to ask the third question that you should, that I thought you were going to ask—I am not talking about the risks of bioengineering, of genetic engineering, etcetera. There is definitely an enormous amount of risk in the transgenic, it's something I would shy away from very, very strongly; but what I am trying to get into the debate is whether the risk of eliminating a particular term such as determinism, dualism, what have you, is going to shape what it is that we are doing, or going to have some sort of an impact, on human activity in the future. This is an open question; I do not know the answer. But the risks that I am talking about, are not about the physical risks of practicing biology, but the philosophical risks of divorcing ourselves from determinism.

ELIZABETH (BETSY) ERMARTH: Or embracing determinism.

AVIV BERGMAN: Or embracing determinism.

HELEN LONGINO: Well, that I thought was the pedagogical problem, which is the more general problem.

DAVID BYRNE: I am thinking about the way sociologists and social anthropologists do work, OK, and the term which is popularized by this is reflexivity; you have to be reflexive, you have to engage in something like a double interpretation of the things, the social contexts you are interpreting, but also in the interpretation of the way you yourself are embodied, connected, constructed. And it strikes me that that is very simplistic, but that is kind of a solution to that problem. But there has not been any kind of reflexivity towards this term, but reflexivity is not the same thing as necessary dismissal. It is simply a constant process of questioning.

ALEXEI GRINBAUM: This phrase in the paper, "Theory shapes reality through belief." I wanted to give an example of someone and then to ask the question, why is it? Why does theory shape reality through belief? The example takes place in the Soviet Union at the end of 1945; the war had just ended and in the Soviet Union the attitude is quite open toward Great Britain and in Great Britain toward the Soviet Union. And then suddenly in 1946, the Cold War starts, so everything goes closed. Now at the end of 1945—I hope you will find this example exaggerated; that is what I aim at, although the example is perfectly real. At the end of 1945 Isaiah Berlin, who was not yet Sir Isaiah Berlin, who was just a diplomat at the British Embassy in Moscow, goes to Leningrad and meets Anna Akhmatova, the great Russian poetess, and talks with her. He is only the second foreigner whom Akhmatova has seen since the Revolution, basically. And he talks with her for hours and hours and hours and then goes back to England and, well, disappears. And Akhmatova wrote several poems, two poems, dedicated to this conversation with Berlin. That is all. Well, what happens is that Akhmatova comes to England in 1965, twenty years later, meets Berlin and says, you know why the Cold War started? Because Stalin learned about our meeting, of course, and got outraged. Now the end of my example is that if you go into Harvard University to the Slavic department, there is a seminar on the Cold War, Russian and American literatures of the Cold War, and that seminar has taught that the origin of the Cold War was this meeting. Now theory shapes reality through belief. And the question is well, why does it happen so? I think that there are a bunch of cognitive barriers which prevent human beings from going somewhere else, from beliefs to, you know, rational analysis. The fact that there are barriers is not bad; there are barriers, well, let us live with it. Barriers simply mean that there is sort of laziness. What does laziness mean? There is incoming information, there is a blinding, what I would call a blinding influence of incoming information that means that a human being usually takes information and acts on it quickly without questioning the information.

IVAR EKELAND: When I said theory should shape belief I always think of something very precise in fact. Namely, you can see the whole of economics as the problem of coordination. How do you coordinate behaviors from diverse individuals, situations of equilibrium and so on and so forth? So the main problem of economics is coordination. One way is through a commonly held belief, and this is not seen as a paradox in that case as a way of commonly held beliefs that the sun, the stars, out there or the spot on the sun will influence, will coordinate behavior.

Organizers' Opening Remarks

Immanuel Wallerstein

We know, or think we know, that our ancestors living, say, 20,000 years ago were in search of explanations of what happened in the world—what happened with great frequency to be sure, but also of what happened rarely (say, a great flood). They came up with explanations, so we are told, that we would call in the language of today "magical explanations." X happened because the gods willed it, or it happened because a witch wanted it to happen. And if we then asked why the gods or a witch did things to make it happen, we often came up with scapegoats among our fellows. The gods or the witch acted because some of us did Y and, as a result, the gods or the witch acted as they did.

Now what good were these explanations about what happened? It seems to me that the psychology of this search for explanations is that the deterministic explanations permitted agency. Far from agency being the opposite of necessity, it was necessity that seemed to validate agency. If we know that X happens in a certain way, then perhaps we can do things to avert it. To take a current example, if we know that a certain disease is caused by W, then perhaps we can develop a vaccine to extinguish W or to remedy W or to minimize the impact of W. It is only when we are certain about necessity that, we seem to think, we can affect necessity and invoke an alternative necessity that we prefer.

The search for necessary explanations thus has had a long history, and everywhere on the planet. There are of course alternative metaphysics that have been developed about the necessary. We have theological necessity—as revealed, for example, by sacred texts. Or we have philosophical necessity, as when we discover (intuit?) categorical imperatives or natural laws. And we have scientific certainties (or at least provisional certainties) when we conduct rigorous experiments that are falsifiable and repeatedly verified.

But of course, we also know, as historians of knowledge, that whatever has been put forth as certain has been contested by others at the time, and revised by its proponents (or the heirs of its original proponents) at a later point of time. This is true of theological, philosophical, and scientific certainties. Nothing seems to be less certain than what is proclaimed as certain. Here, at least, the scientists have been the most honest. They admit that their certainties are in theory only provisional, that they will probably later be undone by revised proclamations of certainties. But they also insist, however, on acting in the present as though the current certainties were truly certain. Failing to do so is denounced as folly or madness or at the very least imprudence. It is also denounced as being anti-intellectual.

Now, suppose we took the radical step to accept what Prigogine proclaimed in his last book, that we are living in the era of the "end of certainties." Suppose we believed that we can never, ever be certain about anything. Does that mean that there is then no science? No agency? I do not think so; I believe that there can be a science of the plausible, one that recognizes the limitations of its knowledge in the present (and not only in the future). I believe that we can build an entire world of knowledge on the basis of the inevitability of uncertainty, the necessity, if you will, of uncertainty.

That is what I meant when I previously said that we should get rid of necessity. The complex probable can be considered the most plausible. We can analyze on the basis of the most plausible; we can make moral choices on the basis of the most plausible. And we can act in the real world on the basis of what is most plausible. Not that we will all agree on what is most plausible—of course not. But the debate about relative plausibility becomes then the real scientific debate. And while only superspecialists can have useful perceptions about the details of very specific phenomena, it is not true that knowledge is the domain of the specialists. For when we put all the superspecialist details into one complex analysis, then we are all more or less equally capable of judging whether the whole seems plausible to us.

We will then have a different knowledge, a different science, but not at all a diminished one. Quite to the contrary, science will be legitimated—not by the latest gadget it makes possible, but by its overall impact on our entire lives over the multiplicity of generations. In such a perspective, determinism is not a very useful concept, and we should spend as much time on it as we do on magic or on astrology.

During the discussion, Steven Fuller distinguished between scientific laws as representative or normative. He said, in effect, that they present themselves as representative but that they function in fact as something that is normative. I certainly believe this is true in the social sciences. I hesitate, out of lack of competence, to generalize this to biology and physics. But I suspect it is true of them as well.

But if this is true, then the requirement of reflexivity, about which David Byrne spoke, is obligatory not merely for anthropologists and sociologists but for all the practitioners of the various forms of knowledge. I look forward to the day when chemists and philosophers will preface their articles with a confession of self-interest. In any case, I look forward to the day when we all think and speak using the so-called intermediate terms—probable/improbable, frequent/infrequent, inclined/disinclined.

There is a price for this, to be sure. The price is paid in terms of the fact that, if everything is uncertain, we cannot be sure that we will win out. The chances become fifty-fifty. And this is a very hard psychological base for action. Before we put energy into action—intellectual, moral, or political action—we like to think we have a good chance that the reward for such effort is the likelihood of success, if not immediately then in the long term.

But the reality is that nothing is determined, everything is uncertain. And the sooner humans learn to live with that reality and function in awareness of all it implies, the sooner we shall create a somewhat livable, somewhat rational world.

Jacques: . . . however reluctantly, I always come back to what my Captain used to say: "Everything which happens to us in this world, good or bad, is written up above. . . ." Do you, Monsieur, know any way of erasing this writing? . . .

The Master: I am wondering about something . . . that is whether your benefactor would have been cuckolded because it was written up above or whether it was written up above because you cuckolded your benefactor?

Jacques: The two were written side by side. Everything was written at the same time. It is like a great scroll which is unrolled little by little.

You can imagine, Reader, to what lengths I might take this conversation on a subject which has been talked about and written about so much for the last two thousand years without getting one step further forward. If you are not grateful to me for what I am telling you, be very grateful for what I am not telling you. . . .

Jacques: . . . it would have to be written on the scroll that Jacques would break his neck on such a day and Jacques would not break his neck. Can you imagine for a moment that that could happen, whoever made the great scroll?

The Master: There are a number of things one could say about that. . . .

Diderot, Jacques the Fatalist

In a conversation like ours, the philosopher's task is at the same time modest and daunting: it consists in seeing to it that concepts are used in as rigorous and consistent a way as possible.

Our friend Fernando Gil has written a rich and fascinating paper about the role, if any, of necessity in human affairs. I am not sure he has really addressed the issue of determinism. It might very well be the case that the world is entirely deterministic without entailing that things and events, most especially human actions, could not be different from what they are. Put in other terms that are as old as metaphysics, it is by no means obvious that determinism and free will are incompatible. Determinism is not the same concept as Necessitarianism, that is to say, the doctrine which asserts that every event that occurs in the world could not be otherwise. It would be an equally serious mistake to confuse determinism and knowability. We all agreed that there are deterministic dynamical processes that are not predictable, even in principle—for instance, "deterministic chaos." Conversely, the outcomes of many random procedures obey the "law of large numbers" and safe bets can be placed about them. The obvious fact that the future is for us, human beings, radically uncertain is no proof that the world is not entirely determined.

I will fly back to Paris on November 26, 2004. This is something Fernando predicted this morning, today being November 21. Fernando is a very good psychologist, he knows me, knows that I have compelling reasons to return to Paris. Besides, I showed him my airline ticket. Does that entail that it is not in my power, even as I am climbing the stairs to the aircraft, to change my mind and decide to stay in San Francisco? Nobody in their right minds would assert so. Let's consider the metaphysical implications of that capacity that I have. On November 26, I can refrain from flying back to Paris; in that event, Fernando's prediction would turn out to be false, although it has been assumed that he is a perfect predictor. My being free entails that I have the *counterfactual* power to render false a correct prediction—a rather innocent power, or so it seems.

Things become awfully more complex if we assume that the predictor is (the philosophers') God. By definition, in contrast with Fernando's finite although remarkable capacities, God is an *essentially* omniscient predictor, i.e., a predictor who is omniscient in all the worlds in which He exists. We further assume that He exists in all the possible worlds we are considering. In the actual world, God predicted eighty years ago that I would fly out from San Francisco to Paris on November 26, 2004. Is it within my power, when the time comes, to refrain from doing that? Let us assume this is the case. In which case, on November 26, I can refrain from flying back to Paris; in that event, God, being omniscient in that possible world too, would have predicted something different from what He predicted in the actual world. My being free entails that I have a *counterfactual power over the past*—not to be confused with a causal power, which would be hard to make sense of.

Philosophers who tried to defend the compatibility of free will and determinism have been led to that kind of conclusion, ever since this problem was first posed by a contemporary of Aristotle, Diodorus, under the name of "Master Argument."

Isn't the metaphysical price to be paid for driving a wedge between Determinism and Necessitarianism too high? In this respect it is interesting to turn to philosophers who thought that human freedom could only be bought at the price of a belief in a radically non-deterministic world—which belief would have driven someone like Spinoza nuts.

Sartre's philosophy of action is an extreme form of Kantianism. According to his view, there is no reality except in action. Man is nothing else than the ensemble of his acts, nothing else than his life. Reality alone is what counts. A man is involved in life, leaves his print on it, and outside of that there is nothing. In other words, looking back, when death has transformed life into destiny, there are no counterfactuals of the kind: "had I had more time, had the circumstances been different, I would have shown my true worth." *Counterfactuals* of the sort are just cheap excuses.

Freedom is choice. Man is nothing else but what he makes of himself. Man first exists: he is the being who projects himself toward a future and who is conscious of imagining himself as being in the future. Man is a plan which is aware of itself. Nothing exists prior to this plan. There is nothing in heaven.

Once, a student of Sartre came to see him. The time was during the Second World War. His father was a collaborator: his older brother had been killed in 1940, and the young man wanted to avenge him. His mother lived alone with him, very much upset by the treason of her husband and the death of her older son. Sartre's student was her only consolation.

The boy was faced with the choice of leaving for England and joining de Gaulle and the Free French Forces—that is, leaving his mother behind—or remaining with her and helping her to carry on. He was wavering between two kinds of ethics: on the one hand, an ethics of sympathy, of personal devotion; on the other, a broader ethics, but one whose efficacy was more dubious. He had to *choose* between the two.

Who could help him choose? The Christian doctrine? "Love your neighbor": but whom should he love as a neighbor? The fighting man or his mother? Or from a consequentialist perspective, which does the greater good, fighting in a group or helping a particular human being to go on living?

This young man came to Sartre for advice, and Sartre said: You are free, choose, that is, invent. No general ethics can show you what is to be done. There are no omens in the world.

I am not sure I find this kind of "ethics" livable. When one reads such expressions as "I am responsible for everything," and "the peculiar character of human-reality is that it is without excuse," (Sartre 1956, 709) it is hard not to feel to the extreme the very anxiety Sartre tells us is implied by our being free in the world. The limit is reached when Sartre extends the range of freedom to the past and, in particular, to birth: "Thus in a certain sense I *choose* being born" (1956, 710); or else: "In order for us to 'have' a past, it is necessary that we maintain it in existence by our very project toward the future; we do not receive our past, but the necessity of our contingency implies that *we are not able not to choose it*" (1956, 639, my emphasis).

Sartre is here fully indebted to Heidegger's analysis of the historicity of "human-reality" (*Dasein*). For the author of *Sein und Seit*, "in the first place, 'human-reality' is historical in that its essential property is to *choose* what later seems to it to be *destiny*"; and furthermore, "what we call '*destiny*' is thus the 'resolved-decision' (*Entschlossenheit*) of 'human-reality.' " Sartre expresses this: "To be finite, in fact, is to choose oneself—that is, to make known to oneself what one is by projecting oneself toward one possible to the exclusion of others" (1956, 698).

To bring out the complexity of the issues which are at stake here, it is, I submit, interesting to compare Sartre's philosophy of absolute freedom with what seems to be its extreme opposite, a conception of the world in which human beings are submitted to a merciless Fate. If we discover that strange resonances unite them, I may ask you, like Diderot, to imagine to what lengths I might take this conversation. I am thinking of Max Weber's famous thesis on the "correlations" between the "Protestant ethic," or more exactly the ethical consequences of the doctrine of predestination, and the "spirit of capitalism." I am interested only in the logical structure of Weber's argument, not in its empirical validity. In virtue of a divine decision taken for all eternity, each person belongs to a group, that of the elect or that of the damned, without knowing which. There is no way to affect this decree, nothing one can do to earn or merit salvation. Divine grace, however, manifests itself through *signs*. What is important is that these signs cannot be observed through introspection: they are acquired through action. The main sign is the success one obtains by putting one's faith to the test in a professional activity (*Beruf*). This test is costly. It requires one work ceaselessly, methodically, without ever resting secure in, without ever enjoying, one's wealth. "Unwillingness to work," Weber notes, "is symptomatic of the lack of grace" (1985, 159).

The "logical consequence" of this practical problem, Weber notes again, "obviously" should have been "fatalism." Fatalism, in other words the choice of an idle life, is in effect the rational solution since, *whatever the state of the world—* here, that one is of the elect or of the damned—one has nothing to win by engaging in the costly test of professional commitment. In decision theory, one is said to be dealing with a "dominant" strategy, in the sense that it is the best one in each possible case. As we know, however, Weber's whole book attempts to explain why and how "the broad mass of ordinary men" has made the opposite choice.

The popular Calvinist doctrine held it "to be an absolute duty to consider oneself chosen, and to combat all doubts as temptations of the devil, since lack of self-confidence is the result of insufficient faith, hence of imperfect grace" (Weber 1985, 111). "Intense worldly activity" was what allowed one to obtain this self-confidence, the means to assure oneself of one's state of grace.

This paradoxical Calvinist choice might be dubbed "choosing one's predestination." Just as "when Adam took the apple it would have been *possible* for him not to take it" (Sartre 1956, 602), when the Calvinist makes the Calvinist choice, it would have been possible for him to make the opposite choice. Just as there would then have been another Adam, there would have been another Calvinist; instead of being chosen, he would have been damned. The example of Adam and the apple is, as we recall, the one that Sartre uses in order to distinguish his position from that of Leibniz. According to the latter, Adam's essence is not chosen by Adam, but by God. His freedom is thus only illusory. According to Sartre, to the contrary, Adam's existence precedes his essence. Free Adam chooses himself: His existence determines his essence, "henceforth what makes his *person* known to him is the future and not the past; he chooses to learn what he is by means of ends toward which he projects himself" (1956, 603). The Calvinist follows Leibniz and Sartre at the same time. His essence determines his existence, but, since he is free to choose his existence, he can determine his essence. He has, literally, the power to choose his predestination. However, as Plantinga insists, this power is not causal—which would make it inconceivable since causality would then fly counter to the arrow of time. It is a "*counterfactual* power over the past."

The subject, knowing himself to be free, reasons thus: If I make this choice, rather than the opposite choice, this action would be the *sign* that I am in a certain world, with its past, its *determinism*, my essence specific to this world. If I chose to act differently, I would be in another world and my essence would be different. It is not that my action causally determines my world: it *reveals* it. However, since I am free *and* rational, my choice must satisfy an external principle: it must maximize my utility, pleasure, happiness—any one of these terms is applicable here, for one readily accepts that the Calvinist prefers eternal salvation to damnation, even if this salvation is acquired at the price of a life of labor. I thus choose to acquire the signs of my salvation—without, however, considering that I thus *cause* my salvation by buying it.

The tension in which Sartre's concept of freedom is situated, between a Spinozan model of acquiescence to a pre-established necessity and a Kantian model of absolute autonomy, is in a way brought into play by the Calvinist choice: the simultaneousness of acquiescing to destiny and producing this destiny oneself. We are dealing entirely with what Fernando Gil called "intermediate concepts," or, quoting Goethe, "mobile order."[1]

NOTE

1. May Fernando, whose beautiful contribution to our conference may have been one of his last intellectual interventions, rest in peace.

REFERENCES

Sartre, Jean-Paul. 1957. *Existentialism and Human Emotions.* (Orig. 1945). New York: Philosophical Library.
Sartre, Jean-Paul. 1956. *Being and Nothingness,* trans. by Hazel E. Barnes. (Orig. 1943). New York: Philosophical Library.
Weber, Max. 1985. *The Protestant Ethic and the Spirit of Capitalism,* trans. by Talcott Parsons. (Orig. 1904). London: Allen & Unwin.

DISCUSSION

BOAVENTURA DE SOUSA SANTOS: I am a bit puzzled by the dynamics of this group; my interest is to see what basic things we agree on at this point. They are probably more important than the things on which we disagree. I think that from my point of view, at least for the social science point of view, I would like to understand the world in a way that enables me to change it for the better. If understanding the world has to be developed at the cost of paralyzing me, I do not like that kind of understanding. So I would like both to understand it and contribute to a change for the better. Second point is that I fully agree with Immanuel [Wallerstein], and I think most people here would agree, that the general mood of this group is there are limits to our knowledge. Jean-Pierre [Dupuy] is right that if these limits are necessary then necessity comes in in our discussions. We cannot get rid of them in practice. But then everything would be solved if we would agree on the kinds of limits of our knowledge. The problem is that we are probably divided on the specific limits of our knowledge. But there are features that may be enabling for some and constraining for others. For instance, for Immanuel [Wallerstein] and for myself I think, metaphysics is constraining because of the ways in which we look into the past; in fact the metaphysical, theological, or whatever, bias, concepts or whatever you may call them, have led us to some major disasters, and we want to avoid that. But from Jean-Pierre [Dupuy]'s point of view metaphysics is enabling, not constraining.

JEAN-PIERRE DUPUY: Exactly.

BOAVENTURA DE SOUSA SANTOS: But then I am concerned that there are things I do not understand because if this metaphysics is agent-based then it is based on choices or range of choices, as Immanuel [Wallerstein] was saying. Then the possible should be a key concept; emphasis should be on the possible, not on the necessary. Because I think we cannot get rid of the necessity if it is the necessity of the limits of looking at necessity. So if our knowledge of necessity is necessarily immediate, of course we do not get rid of necessity, but our research energies should be in fact focused on the possible—on avoiding Auschwitz and embracing World Social Forums.

JEAN-PIERRE DUPUY: It is a question of strategy. I fully agree with you that what is important is to change the world. I think our world is heading directly in the direction of major catastrophe, which has many facets: global warming, terrorism, radical inequalities. We must change that. I fully agree with you that we have to choose the right metaphysics in order to wage that war, not of terror, but against the major catastrophes that are about to occur. It is a matter of strategy. So now the question is which metaphysics is most appropriate for this fight? Which I think I understand we share. So the point where we are now in the history of humankind suggests the strategy that consists in believing that the future is open, it branches out, and we have to fight in order to find the right branch, the one that avoids the catastrophe. The major obstacle to our avoiding the catastrophe is not that we lack knowledge—it is that we know many things, but that we do not manage ourselves to believe what we know. We have the knowledge but it is not transformed into belief. The catastrophe is not fatal. Who among us really believes in the catastrophe in terms of global warming? Certainly not in this country. So we have to transform knowledge into belief. And for me this is of course a political problem. But there is no politics without ethics and there is no ethics without metaphysics. So in terms of urgency politics comes first, then ethics, then metaphysics. It is more important to change the world than to understand it, but it is absolutely necessary, if I can use this word, to understand it. And then metaphysics comes first and then ethics and then politics. Now just one word about metaphysics: I think it is absolutely necessary in strategic terms for us to believe that the catastrophe is inscribed in the future. That we have to believe that in order for it not to occur. Because it is only if we believe that catastrophe is inscribed in the future that we find the means [to avert it].

IMMANUEL WALLERSTEIN: And if we believe it is probable?

JEAN-PIERRE DUPUY: No, it is not enough. We have to believe that it is really inscribed in the future.

IMMANUEL WALLERSTEIN: Where do you get that empirically?

JEAN-PIERRE DUPUY: Ah! But metaphysics is not empirical.

IMMANUEL WALLERSTEIN: Yes, but I want to know where you get empirically the assertion that if people believe that something is probable they will not act to avert it.

JEAN-PIERRE DUPUY: Oh, that is the global warming. Except that as I said they do not believe what they know, but they know it. They have the knowledge.

JOÃO CARAÇA: But the basic alternative is not that catastrophe is inscribed in the future, it is that it is already here.

JEAN-PIERRE DUPUY: Yes, yes.

JOÃO CARAÇA: The problem can be about modulating the direction.

JEAN-PIERRE DUPUY: I agree.

JOHN MARTIN FISHER: During the break I was talking with Immanuel [Waller-stein] and I found that it seems as though we were in agreement because I think he said, correct me if I'm wrong, that it's not so much that you're concerned to completely illuminate the conceptual category of necessity or the necessary, but the main point is that we should take it off its throne, take it off its high horse. I think we can all agree on that. To think of it as hegemonic or dominant or the only real possibility is problematic in distorting a lot of ways, but I think my overall message, if I have one, as a philosopher, especially an analytic philosopher, I always believe that when you are in doubt, make a distinction [laughter]. But I think we have to really avoid talking about necessity and possibility without distinguishing different kinds of necessity, different kinds of possibilities, and taking a more nuanced view of what kind of methodology is appropriate for which subject matters. So for instance, we in philosophy would distinguish logical necessity from metaphysical necessity, and of course physical necessity and causal necessity, causal necessity given the past necessity per accidents from Occam and that temporally indexed necessity that Jean-Pierre [Dupuy] was talking about, epistemic necessity. There are all these different notions and we need to be more careful, more nuanced in our application of them. Also I think we need to study carefully the logic of explanation and take seriously the idea that it is local and that for certain phenomena, certain kinds of explanation are appropriate and for other phenomena other kinds are appropriate. And they all may involve a combination of necessity and contingency or change. So I would take the more nuanced approach.

JOHN CASTI: Just to comment on what you just said, Jean-Pierre [Dupuy], about translating the technology into belief, if you like. I think that one can construct lots of examples where we have knowledge and people even believe it, but from beliefs then you want to go another step to action. And one thing you didn't mention and I think is part of the nuancing is the issue of time scale. For example, I think we can all understand the fact that this whole planet is going to get burned up in about six billion years or thereabouts when the sun expands. But nobody is worrying about it. And nobody is taking any action about that because it is too far away. It is hopelessly remote as far as any human time scale is concerned. Now suppose that we have the knowledge that some meteorite was out there on a path coming to crash into the earth in a month's time, two months time, whatever it might be. We would believe it, and among some people, a lot of resources would be immediately mobilized to try and do something about that. I do not think you would have to go through the metaphysics to the ethics to the politics to get to that academic point. Global warming is somewhere sort of in-between. And this is the in-between case. It is difficult and like the mid-game in chess, that is the interesting part. And so these time scales matter a lot as far as your hierarchy of steps to go through to action which changes the situation.

JEAN-PIERRE DUPUY: Yes, yes, I agree.

V. BETTY SMOCOVITIS: On a related point, Jean-Pierre [Dupuy], what exactly counts as catastrophic?

JEAN-PIERRE DUPUY: It is a matter of nuances.

V. BETTY SMOCOVITIS: There are more people who die as a result of smoking per year than died in 9/11. I mean I am not quite clear on the statistics exactly but I have seen some of them. What do you mean, what do we mean by catastrophic exactly? And the other point, it is a complicating element, I know, but in this room we keep talking about the human condition. And I would suggest that our discussion has been very anthropocentric. I am part of a unit in zoology where people actually want to see things like, or they believe that emerging viruses, infectious diseases, things like SARS are actually part of the natural order of things.

And this is the planet's way, I'm not saying I support this view, but this is the planet's way of, it is a kind of biological catharsis. If human beings are in fact the worst things that have happened to the planet earth, this is actually—

JEAN-PIERRE DUPUY: Something to worry about—

V. BETTY SMOCOVITIS: And so I really think you need to factor in nonhuman actors as you think about what counts as a catastrophe. I think of things like the destruction of the rain forest, I worry about global warming. Look, I am with you; if I were to list ten catastrophic events, I would probably come up with a list very much like yours. But I do think you want to think about what counts as catastrophic as you try to avert catastrophe and develop strategies and so on. Listen, if you were to ask a group of Republicans what counts as catastrophic, they would say gay marriage. It's context driven.

IMMANUEL WALLERSTEIN: You listed 9/11 as a catastrophe. I do not think it was a catastrophe at all. I think it is a minor event, a minor event in the modern history of the world. I have written this. I believe it. It comes out of an analysis that I have of the state of the modern world-system and what is going on. So the first problem we have is to have a debate about social reality and therefore to be able to assess what are serious problems. For example, I am worried about the next 50 years. And I think I can make a case; I have made it, but I am not going to give it to you now, of what's going to happen in the next 50 years and what the choices are before us. 9/11 plays no role in that. Terrorism plays no role in that. But other things play very big roles in that. Bifurcation going on, and there is a major collective choice going on in the next 50 years. And I want it to go in one direction. Other people want it to go in another direction and this is a moral choice about moral values, right? And then that leads me to political conclusions. If I decide that I want to go in X direction rather than Y direction, then I have to develop a political strategy that will push the world in one direction rather than the other direction. I can also come to the issue of why we are debating determinism. I can explain that in terms of the structures of knowledge and their role in the modern world-system and the fact that I think the modern world-system is in a structural crisis and part of the structural crisis is to raise questions about the structures of knowledge which sustain the system; that is why it is occurring today and did not occur 50 or 100 years ago in this form. There were no such meetings about these kinds of epistemological questions then. That is all part of what is going on. And that is why I also think that the discourse that we develop now is going to affect the political and moral choices that we will make in the next 50 years. It is not an abstract question. It is not a question of truth. I am setting it within the structure of social science, a social science analysis of the realities of the world in which we are living. And you are giving us things, which are in that sense universalistic. You are giving us analyses that are presumably available over all points of time and so forth and I am trying to say, no, we are dealing with a very concrete and empirical reality. It is very large scale, very important. And global warming is part of it and I can explain why we are having global warming which is politically based. There were fundamental choices that were made and are continuing to be made that are leading to a physical phenomenon, which is global warming. And the fact that people are not excited about global warming is also politically based. The pressures to suppress discussion of global warming are clear, particularly in the U.S. but in other parts of the world as well. And that is very efficacious, and these become major political issues. And there are metaphysical assumptions that are going on and that leads me to be concerned with the structures of knowledge and the choices that are being made today and in the next 10, 15, 20 years about the structures of knowledge which have been questioned for all sorts of reasons and that is what the book, *Open the Social Sciences*, and other books that I have been involved in, were about. These are a collectivity of things we have to agree on; we have to have a substantive discussion about social reality, its present state, and the likely directions in which it is moving. I have to persuade you that we are at a point where the system cannot maintain itself and it's far from equilibrium and is about to collapse and therefore is in a bifurcation. And then I have to say yes, then we have moral decisions to be made and we have to come to some kind of collective discussion about what is a catastrophe. That is an important, major question. It has no self-evident answer.

AVIV BERGMAN: And I think that we need to discuss what we mean by epistemology in the social sciences, what we mean by epistemology in the philosophical arena, and what it means to me as a scientist.

IMMANUEL WALLERSTEIN: You do not think it means the same thing in all cases?

AVIV BERGMAN: No, you are looking at it from a practical point of view. I am looking at it from a practical point of view and I have no stakes in it. But Jean-Pierre [Dupuy] is looking at it from an ethical point of view with everything staked on it.

IMMANUEL WALLERSTEIN: I have stakes in it. We are together on that. We have stakes in it.

AVIV BERGMAN: No, but you are using it as a mechanism to predict; he is not using it as a mechanism to predict.

IMMANUEL WALLERSTEIN: Then I predict. I do my best to predict in order to make the moral decisions. So I have great stakes in it. I just think I need to create the range of possibilities, the realistic range of possibility at the present moment in order to make my moral decisions. I have a stake in the fact that the historical system in which we are all living is in my view coming to a collapse and it's going to move in one of two different directions and I am concerned which of the two different directions it takes.

AVIV BERGMAN: So what does the epistemological concept of determinism have to do with it?

IMMANUEL WALLERSTEIN: It has everything to do with it because it assumes that all systems, all physical systems, all biological systems, all social systems move far from equilibrium. When they move far from equilibrium then they can no longer operate within whatever structural framework they have and then they bifurcate and they can go in one of two possible directions, or perhaps more than that, and that in historical social systems there is an element of human choice that is operating as to whether they go in one direction or another. That is the epistemology that underlies my argument and that affects my concern with the structures of knowledge and therefore affects my concern with such issues as discourse, which is almost a minor question, but it is important to dethrone a set of assumptions which operated fairly well within the existing historical system for a good 200 years but which are cramping us enormously in appreciating the reality of the world in which we are now living, and therefore what the real choices are before us and therefore what might enable us to move in one direction or another.

IVAR EKELAND: I prefer the way Immanuel [Wallerstein] is taking the question than you, Jean-Pierre [Dupuy], so I will translate what you said in my language, not words, in a way I said that we can say this is a question of choice, of preferences, collective preferences. Global warming is bad. Why? For whom? I just don't see how you can say that one set of ethics is better than another. From what point of view? It may be the case that from the point of view of this particularly nasty species infecting this planet and so there are some observers that say, well, is that a chance let us get away with it. It makes a perfectly sensible metaphysic position. So in other words, how can you say that a set of metaphysics is better than another? I just don't see it.

STEVE FULLER: It is true we have been taking for granted at the object level that whatever else we want to do, we want to preserve the human species. We might have different ways of doing it but that is kind of what we all want to do. But in fact the future is more open than that. And this is the move now to the general metaphysical framework within which we can understand what most of us may regard as complete catastrophe, where large numbers of human beings are eliminated through AIDS and other viruses and disease organisms. From an alternative standpoint, it would be regarded as a way of the planet purging itself and getting back to a more holistic vision. Now were we to go down the latter route, then this would have a sort of feedback effect in terms of how we would have understood our paths and having gotten there. So for example, the old Nazi science of racial hygiene was predicated exactly on this idea that human beings in a sense were potentially a blight on the planet and there was a lot of hostility to things like immunology and things that kept people alive artificially and so forth within Nazi Germany and in fact within the ten-year period before that. This science is totally discredited now, because we believe in the preservation of human beings as a kind of end in itself. But if we do change the value assumptions down the road and we start getting more tolerant of this idea of humans being eliminated and so forth, then this will have a feedback effect in terms of how we understand the past history of science. Then we would say something like, "had racial hygiene been allowed to flourish, perhaps had we reached political settlement with the Nazis earlier on, so they would not have had to go to the extreme of the Holocaust and had racial hygiene been allowed to develop more fully as a science, then in fact we could have gotten to the state where half the human population was gone much earlier." In which case, then the normative state of Nazism and racial hygiene will have changed. To explain this phenomenon which might well happen in the future, so in other words, if we go down the route of the anti-humanistic zoologists, then we will end up with a feedback mechanism that will cause us to reinterpret what the past has been, in which case something like Nazism will probably not look so bad. I think it's only when you adopt a metaphysical framework like Jean-Pierre [Dupuy]'s that you can actually start to come to grips with that possibility. Which is, I think, a possibility that has a certain degree of probability to it if we go down 50–100 years from now.

IMMANUEL WALLERSTEIN: You are saying the past always changes. I agree.

STEVE FULLER: No, but you do need a framework like that as a second order in order to get a grip on this. You know where the future is changing the past.

V. BETTY SMOCOVITIS: Analogies break down at some point and I think you have stretched it with the zoologists and Nazis a bit far, because where there is a difference is that what the Nazis were doing was culling and creating.

STEVE FULLER: Racial hygiene existed 50 years before the Nazis.

V. BETTY SMOCOVITIS: But whoever it happened to be, this is not what I was trying to describe. I think I want you to rethink this.

STEVE FULLER: If you look at the racial hygiene literature, it was very sophisticated. In fact, the founder was nominated for the Nobel Prize in 1936. And the Nazis in a sense gave this movement a bad name, you might say. And it is coming back.

V. BETTY SMOCOVITIS: The notion of betterment is not what I have in mind here. They are not culling humans into superior and inferior.

STEVE FULLER: No, they are letting nature do it.

V. BETTY SMOCOVITIS: No, not nature; you are reading into it. They are saying if all *Homo sapiens* disappear, this is not saying there are elite and superior forms of life. They are saying *Homo sapiens* as a whole is bad news for the planet.

IMMANUEL WALLERSTEIN: Because that is what is creating global warming.

V. BETTY SMOCOVITIS: And the other thing that you must recognize is they are acknowledging the power relationship between us and nonhuman agents. So it is linked up to the, I don't want to call it the animal rights movement because rights is a loaded term, but we are looking at allowing nonhuman actors to give them a—

STEVE FULLER: The racial hygiene people had all this—

V. BETTY SMOCOVITIS: But they are not trying to create inferior and superior—

STEVE FULLER: They do not have to; they think nature is going to do it. I'm not talking about the superior. I'm talking about the business, the idea that viruses, these mass viruses, the epidemics, serve a function with regard to bringing a kind of whole to nature, that in fact you may go overboard in trying to immunize people against disease.

V. BETTY SMOCOVITIS: No, no, no, you are reading into it. That sounds like going back to Darwin like a descent of man and that is not what I am talking about here. This is a radical environmentalism that does not have humans in the picture. It is really different. It is really different. Again, I lived part of my life in this tropical environment where people say these things. They are ecologists. By the way, while we are on the subject of systems, could you try to sort of think of systems in terms of ecosystems?

IMMANUEL WALLERSTEIN: Sure.

V. BETTY SMOCOVITIS: I mean we are really not talking about environments when we have these discussions of globalities. It is all human-oriented technology. We do not have the desert, we do not have all this other stuff in it and I think it ought to be factored in at some point.

IMMANUEL WALLERSTEIN: Well, I factor it in, surely, but all these ecosystem changes are the result, a very large part of it, is the result of human social decisions of various kinds. So the ecosystem becomes therefore almost a part of the human social system rather that the human social system being a part of the ecosystem.

DAVID BYRNE: I think this is an extraordinarily useful and constructive in all kinds of ways. But I think about it picking up on some of the points you made. This is a group to use the Gramscian term "traditional intellectuals." OK, that is what we are doing. Perfectly legitimate thing to do, we are embedded in the economy, we are talking about the ideas and the construction of knowledge in the way in which it is constructed but we have not got a connection as such or an explicit connection to the kind of agency business Gramsci was talking about. So we argue correctly about how we actually import virtue, as opposed to evil. We argue correctly about how we actually understand things. We argue about art in terms of the nature and character of action. But we lack the notion of some kind of collective and universal actor to which we could appeal and which we could inform and engage with. I'm a member of the Green Party, which is a very red Green Party, the U.K. Green Party. But there is a dark green green conception from which exactly old Lovelock himself is divorced.

V. BETTY SMOCOVITIS: I was thinking of Lovelock.

DAVID BYRNE: How do the kinds of arguments we have here enter into that more general debate? They enter into it traditionally because they inform the way in which we teach our students and inform the nature of knowledge as a practice within our kind of society, but that is a very slow way. It is a long way. It does not have the direct connection to what is happening in the World Social Forum. So those are the questions I take away. I do not expect anybody to answer those questions.

IMMANUEL WALLERSTEIN: Why don't we use that as a closing statement?

INDEX

Accidents, 70

Action: chance and necessity in, 69; choice and, 69, 123; collective emergent property of, 87; consequences of, 123; deliberation and, 69; divine, 12; free, 48; human, 4, 69, 145; moral judgments on, 86; necessity and, 75, 79; organized knowledge and, 10; philosophy of, 168; potential for, 10; rational, 1–2, 5; representation and, 56; social, 50, 60; theory of, 149; uncertainty and, 69; voluntary, 76, 85

Agency, 63; moral, 9; rational, 135; validation through necessity, 3, 163

Ainslie, George, 34n3

Akhmatova, Anna, 160

Alchemy, 13, 25

Alienation, 101

Allan, Peter, 89

Anticipation: in economic theory, 123; self-fulfilling, 128

Aporia, 67, 68; constitutive, 68

Aristotle, 37n17, 69, 88; on causality, 71, 72, 73, 88, 89; chance/necessity polarity and, 2; on contingency, 75; *Eudemian Ethics*, 75; *On Generation and Corruption*, 75; intermediate figures of, 2; *Magna Moralia*, 70, 74; *Metaphysics*, 72, 76; on necessary actions, 79; *Nicomachean Ethics*, 69; on non-necessity,

75–77; *Organon*, 76; *Prior Analytics*, 75; *Rhetoric*, 75; treatment of chance and necessity, 67, 71, 72, 73, 74

Astrology, 20

Axioaetiotics, 38n20

Bacon, Francis, 27

Bacon, Roger, 11, 13

Baker, Keith, 45, 56, 92, 94, 95, 96, 105, 110, 148

Bayesian approach to economic theory, 3, 123, 125, 127

Behavior: collective, 130; conforming, 135; cooperative, 11; determinants of, 131; individual, 130, 131; mathematical models of, 117, 118; modifying, 131

Being and Nothingness (Sartre), 48

Beliefs, 3; constructed, 150; coordinating, 129; equilibrium approach modeling formation of, 127–129; formation of, 3, 123, 125, 127; initial, 3, 123, 125, 126, 133; knowledge transformed into, 10, 174; modeling, 127; reality shaping and, 160; technology translated into, 175

Belkin, Aaron, 29

Bergman, Aviv, 52, 54, 57, 60, 98, 99, 143, 148, 149, 150, 151, 159, 179

Berlin, Isaiah, 160

Bernal, J.D., 35n7

Berofsky, Bernard, 7
Biology: as connector of social science and physical science, 58; determinism in, 121–122; evolutionary, 159; functional, 57; historical, 57; lack of interest in determinism in, 63
Bioprospecting, 37n16
Bohr, Niels, 60
Bouveresse, Jacques, 78
Brave New World (Huxley), 11
Buridan, Jean, 34n3
Buridan's donkey, 127
Byrne, David, 41, 50, 58, 83, 86, 93, 97, 103, 105, 111, 113, 141, 142, 144, 160, 184

Calvinism, 3, 96, 97, 170, 171
Capitalism, 14, 158, 170
Caraça, João, 60, 87, 111, 141, 155, 174, 175
Casti, John, 43, 44, 51, 52, 54, 83, 86, 132, 133, 137, 146, 147, 148, 175
Catastrophe, 176, 177, 179; defining, 4
Causality: in economics, 124; efficient, 89; final, 89; formal, 89; probabilistic, 108, 109; types of, 88, 89
Cause: of the accidental, 71, 72, 73; chance and, 71; configurational, 50; full knowledge of, 72, 73; proper, 73
Certainty, 164
Chance: exclusion from sphere of comprehension, 70; existence of, 70; as force of destiny, 80; intrinsic legality of, 73; as invention of liberty, 79; laws of, 73; mastery of, 78; necessity and, 2; network of meanings of, 67–83; noume-

nal causality of, 71; opacity of, 72; in opera, 80–83; as opposite of contingent, 75; as opposite of order and uniformity, 74, 75; opposition to necessity, 67; possibility and, 74; powerlessness in the face of, 80; probability theory and, 73; reality of, 71; role of, 67; as surface effect, 71; unintelligibility of, 70
Change: in concept of time, 54; lack of effect on basic constituents, 115; in modality, 32; in the past, 32; in technology, 52; by time travellers, 32; of utility functions with time, 3, 123
Chaos, 2, 6fig; complexity and, 87; as creation of nonlinearity, 87; deterministic, 167; as intermediate concept, 74; theory, 67, 74, 117, 120, 140; underdeterminism and, 16
Choice, 143; freedom as, 168; moral, 164
Chomsky, Noam, 24, 112
Christianity: over/underdeterminism in, 36n13
The Church: authority of, 13; Enlightenment challenges to, 13
Class: knowledge and, 14; social, 14
Communication: with extraterrestrial intelligence, 55; intersubjective, 102; meaningful, 56; necessary conditions for, 109; with other organisms, 56
Complementarity, 54, 57, 60, 61; chaos and, 87; difficulty of disaggregating a system from environment, 87; of freedom and determinism, 2, 5; in physics, 59
Complexity, 2, 52; genesis of, 88; open systems and, 87

Compulsion, necessity and, 76
Comte, Auguste, 10, 11, 122
Configuration, results through, 50
Consequentialism, 86
Constructivism, 9
Contingency, 74, 75, 76; ethics and, 86;
time and, 2, 86; underdeterminism and,
18
Control: determinism and, 3, 131
Conventionalism, 9
Copernicus, Nicolaus, 20
Coumet, Ernest, 73
Culture: formation of, 151

Darwin, Charles, 9, 34*n1*, 122
Daston, Lorraine, 73
Deconstruction: of freedom/determination
binary, 6
Democracy: institutionalization of, 12
Dennett, Daniel, 7
de Olaso, Ezequiel, 77
Derrida, Jacques, 106, 150, 152
Descartes, Rene, 20
de Sousa Santos, Boaventura, 49, 60, 91,
99, 106, 145, 158, 172, 173
Destiny, 169; assertion from within, 81;
chance as force of, 80; local determinisms and, 82
Determinism: absolute end of, 56; agency
and, 163; appropriateness of, 148; as
basis for prediction, 141; belief that
information is neither created nor
destroyed, 115–116; biological, 57;
causality associated with, 45, 51, 88,
117, 121; certainty and, 61; classical,
123, 129, 143; complementarity with

freedom in scientific worldview, 5–33;
control and, 3, 131; dependence on
freedom, 6; disciplinary, 59; economic,
78; economic theory and, 139; elimina-
tion of, 3, 143; emergence from experience, 117; emergence from particular
narratives, 46; evolutionary worldview
and, 6, 6*fig*; expressed in differential
equations, 118, 141; extent of, 26; force
of, 153; freedom and, 2; free will and,
7, 8; future states and, 118; historical
perspective and, 15, 57; Kantian, 8, 44,
51; knowability and, 167; knowledge
production and, 2; language in, 153; as
Lavoisier's law applied to information,
115; limits of, 130; Lockean, 8, 44, 51;
mathematical modeling and, 3, 115–
132; mechanical worldview and, 6, 6*fig*;
moral responsibility and, 64; necessity
and, 88, 166–171; Newtonian physical
law type of, 88; opposition to freedom,
5; origination of idea, 117; overlap
and, 45, 47; paradox of, 119; randomness and, 2; relation to predictability,
142–143; as scientific concept, 98;
scientific concern about, 63; simpliciter,
15; in social science, 3; spaces of free
play and, 77, 78; spontaneity and, 77;
status of, 1; stochastic, 74; strategic,
144; truth/falsity of, 51, 134
Development: intervention in, 27; of
knowledge, 2
Diamond, Jared, 47, 57
Dickens, Charles, 35*n7*
Diderot, Denis, 166, 170
The Dilemma of Determinism (James), 51

Diodorus, 168
Divine sensorium, 15
Dualism, 136, 153, 159
Duns Scotus, John, 23, 24, 34n3, 37n17
Dupuy, Jean-Pierre, 1, 3, 38n21, 48, 88, 90, 94, 96, 97, 98, 99, 101, 112, 113, 132, 139, 152, 155, 159, 172, 173, 174, 175, 176, 179
Durkheim, Emile, 79
Dynamical systems, 3

Economic(s): academic, 147; boundaries of, 151; capitalism and, 158; coordination and, 161; determinism, 78; forecasting, 124, 125; human action and, 145; mathematical model in, 115–132, 141, 146; motion in, 142; nature of indeterminism in, 3; neoclassical, 134, 138, 145, 152; political, 31; power of, 3, 156; rail transport and, 28, 29; slavery and, 30, 31; theoretical, 122; theory, 3, 123, 124, 125, 137, 139; welfare, 137
Ecosystems, 4
Einstein, Albert, 22, 32, 53, 107
Ekeland, Ivar, 3, 132, 133, 136, 137, 138, 142, 146, 151, 180
Elias, Norbert, 50
Elster, Jon, 26
Emergence, 89
Empiricism, 106
Enlightenment: challenges to Church in, 13; freedom to will mentality in, 13; interrelations of history and science in, 12; stage theory of human development in, 13–14; stigmatization of medieval period in, 13

Equilibrium: in systems, 180
Erlich, Paul, 58
Ermarth, Elizabeth, 53, 54, 59, 62, 88, 106, 109, 112, 149, 150, 151, 152, 156, 159
Essentialism: strategic, 144, 153
Eudemian Ethics (Aristotle), 75
Eugenics, 63, 181, 182. See also Racial hygiene policies
Euporia, 68
Existentialism, 34n3
Expectations: changes in, 123; determining, 134; fundamental role of, 139; margins of freedom and, 78; rational, 3, 127–129, 132, 140; referral to future distributions by, 78
Experience: conditions of, 107; emergence of determinism from, 117; learning from, 123; of the tragic, 101; understanding, 2
Explanation, 163; logic of, 175

Falsification principle, 37n17
Fatalism, 6fig, 8, 170; overdeterminism and, 16
Fichte, Johann Gottlieb, 71
Fisher, John Martin, 45, 46, 48, 51, 64, 95, 98, 100, 111, 112, 113, 134, 134sf136, 175
Fogel, Robert, 2, 28, 29, 30, 31
Foucault, Michel, 22, 107
Freedom: absolute, 169; to action, 48; as choice, 168; circumscribing, 35n5; complementarity with determinism in scientific worldview, 5–33; dependence on determinism, 2, 6; evolutionary

worldview and, 6, 6*fig*; God's point of view and, 8; of invention, 79; margins of, 77, 78; mechanical worldview and, 6, 6*fig*; of/to will, 7, 34*n3*, 48; over/underdeterminist views of, 37*n14*; past actions and, 86; personal, 117; philosophy of, 3; rational, 7; as recognition of necessity, 7; valueof, 37*n14*

Freedom/determinism binary. *See also* Determinism; Freedom: attempts at deconstruction of, 6; discussion, 40–65; possible worlds as microstructure of, 25–33; as problem of historical perspective, 15–25

Fuller, Steve, 1, 5–33, 35*n5*, 35*n7*, 36*n10*, 37*n15*, 38*n20*, 40, 42, 44, 46, 48, 62, 63, 88, 91, 112, 113, 134, 134sf136, 135, 136, 145, 152, 155, 156, 165, 180, 182, 183

Future(s): alternative, 49; narratives and, 56; predicting, 53; surety of, 50

Galileo, 20, 104

Game theory, 3, 127, 129–130; equilibrium concept in, 129–130; predictive power and, 129

Genetic(s), 86; designer babies and, 35*n5*; engineering, 122; probabilistic understanding of, 63

Gil, Fernando, 2, 45, 57, 67–83, 86, 88, 91, 92, 93, 96, 166, 171

Global warming, 173, 176, 177, 178, 180

God: exact location of, 15; foreknowledge of decisions by, 97; free will and, 96; innocence of, 116; laws of governance, 12; Newtonian view on role of, 95, 96;

omnipotence of, 96, 138, 139; as predictor, 167; prohibitions of, 7; as social concept, 138; standing equidistant from all history, 15

Godel, Escher, Bach (Hofstadter), 43

Götterdammerung (Wagner), 82, 83

Governance: as closed system, 11; by God, 12; intellectual barriers in, 11; lack of distance to those governed, 12; secrets of effective, 12; systems of, 11

Grinbaum, Alexei, 49, 53, 54, 55, 59, 98, 102, 103, 108, 109, 160

Guns, Germs, and Steel (Diamond), 47

Habermas, Jürgen, 9, 35*n5*, 36*n9*

Hacking, Ian, 73, 78, 79

Heckman, Jim, 125

Hegel, G.W.F., 27, 131; philosophy of history of, 13

Heidegger, Martin, 169

Heisenberg, Werner, 22

History: alternate, 26; discontinuities in, 41; exact understanding of, 28; interdependency of causal and value judgments in significance, 30; lack of ending, 49; narrative of, 46; necessity of all events in, 25; overlap of past and present, 23, 24; philosophy of, 46; possibility in, 42; recurrent, 67; relations of actual and possible events in, 25; relation to science, 2; revisionism and, 31, 32, 33; separation of past and present in, 21; of structures of knowledge, 99, 100; suspension of meaning of the past, 49; trajectories in, 118; of universe, 118

7; of nature, 6, 9, 95, 164; Newton's, 7; normative, 165; providing infrastructure of rational society, 10; representative, 165; scientific, 165; of structure, 89; of three stages, 122; universal, 92

Lee, Richard, 1–4, 142, 144, 145, 146, 149, 153

Leibniz, Gottfried, 37*n17*, 69, 75, 77, 116

Leotard, Jean-Francois, 110

Lévi-Strauss, Claude, 68

Lewis, David, 26, 28, 38*n21*

Lewontin, Richard, 57

Libertarianism, 34*n3*, 38*n21*

Liberty of indifference, 34*n3*

List, Friedrich, 11

Locke, John, 7, 34*n3*, 44, 48

Logic(s): classical, 98; of explanation, 175; of frequency, 77; fuzzy, 98, 99, 111; historical, 2; inductive, 68, 69; modal, 2; nonclassical, 68; partial implication in, 68, 69; of probability, 77; of situations, 20; of values, 111

Longino, Helen, 47, 48, 61, 90, 92, 107, 108, 109, 158, 159, 160

Lucas, Robert, 124, 125

Mach, Ernst, 36*n10*

Machiavelli, Nicolo, 12, 36*n8*

Magna Moralia (Aristotle), 70, 74

Malthus, David, 31

Malthus, Thomas, 156

The Man without Qualities (Musil), 68

Markov chains, 86

Marxism, 8, 30, 60, 78, 145

Materialism, 9

Mathematical models: of behavior, 117, 118; determinism and, 3; dynamical systems, 120; of natural phenomena, 21

Mayr, Ernst, 58

Mechanics: necessitarian, 77, 92; quantum, 52; statistical, 67, 89; universality in, 92

Mechanics, Newtonian, 92; absolute time in, 15

Meno (Plato), 24

Metaphysics: agent-based, 173; alternative, 163; Christianization of, 37*n17*; constraints of, 173; idealist, 25

Metaphysics (Aristotle), 72, 76

Mill, John Stuart, 38*n21*, 135

Modernism: scientific, 6

Moral(s): agency, 9; choices, 164; judgments, 86; responsibility, 5, 64

Motion: differential equations and, 141; in economics, 142; inertial, 20; laws of, 7; in nature, 141; in science, 142; theory of, 149

Multiversum theory, 116

Musil, Robert, 68

Narrative(s): choices of, 57; closed, 52, 56; coherent, 46; of the disciplines, 62; of history, 46; negotiation and, 57; as openings to future, 56; as partial story, 61; reductionistic, 62; sequences, 2, 45; in social science, 52; unifying, 47, 62

National Science Foundation, 14

Naturalism, 9, 35*n5*

Necessitarianism, 69

Necessity, 2; absolute, 75, 96, 98, 104, 111; of action, 75; causal, 175; chance

Plausibility: developing science of, 3
Polanyi, Michael, 24
Popper, Karl, 8, 9, 10, 12, 20, 24, 35n5,
    35n6, 37n17, 78
Positivism, 8; logical, 12, 26
Possibility, 24, 173; alternative, 32, 51;
    chance and, 74; condition of, 109;
    defining, 75; of divine omnipotence, 13;
    illusion and, 5; infinite, 148; necessity
    and, 4, 94, 102; pre-Scotist understand-
    ing of, 24; presuppositions about, 42; of
    probability, 109; semantic sense of, 23;
    temporal sense of, 23; unactualized, 5
Postmodernity, 106
Post-structuralism, 106; challenges to sci-
    ence from, 2
Poverty: natural selection and, 31; welfare
    programs and, 31
The Poverty of Historicism (Popper), 9
Power, 111; causal, 168; counterfactual,
    167, 168, 171; knowledge as, 10,
    12, 14; possibility and, 75, 76;
    redistribution of, 14; spontaneity and,
    77
Pragmatism, 8
Predestination, 97–98, 170
Predictability, 3, 51, 117, 118, 119; rela-
    tion to determinism, 142–143; setting
    conditions for, 141
Predictions, 60; self-fulfilling, 124,
    137
Prigogine, Ilya, 3, 89, 156, 164
Principia (Newton), 124
Principle: of diminishing marginal util-
    ity, 135; of excluded thirds, 111; of
    rationality, 135; of sufficient reason, 71

Prior Analytics (Aristotle), 75
Probability, 106; antimony of, 91;
    attribution of specific functions of,
    85; Bayesian theory and, 3, 123, 125;
    causal chains and, 108; chance and, 73;
    changing with new information, 3, 123,
    125; computing outcomes and, 120;
    conceptual structures, 113; determin-
    istic models, 120; developments in, 2;
    distributions, 147; distributions across
    possibilities, 33; formalization of, 68;
    logic of, 77; necessity and, 67; objective,
    3, 72, 78, 123, 125; one-time events
    and, 3, 123, 125; possibility of, 109;
    shifts in, 31, 32; social science and, 73;
    stochastic models, 120; subjective, 3,
    71, 123, 125, 127; symmetry and, 74;
    taming of chance and, 77; theory, 31,
    73, 74, 78, 84, 119, 120, 123, 137
Protestant Ethic (Weber), 97
Psychophysics, 38n20

Queen of Spades (Tchaikovsky), 81
Quesnay, Francois, 11
Quetelet, Adolphe, 11

Racial hygiene policies, 35n7, 181, 182,
    183
Randomness, 2, 51, 74, 75, 83, 84, 88,
    119, 120
Rational expectations, 51
Rationality: choice of objectives/actions
    in, 122; decision-making and, 130;
    economics theory and, 122, 123;
    formal, 138; principles of, 135;
    substantive, 138

Reality: anthropocentric view of, 7, 8; of chance, 71; describing, 105; epistemological approaches to, 3; existence of, 103; human, 169; metaphysical indeterminism about, 35*n6*; modeling, 122; physical, 32, 124; shaped by theory, 160; social, 177

Reductionism, 124, 134, 136, 153

Reflexivity, 160; requirement of, 165

Relativism, 9

Relativity, general, 21

Representation, performative nature of, 56

Republic (Plato), 12, 14

Research: in applications to improve human condition, 14; change in practices of, 62, 63; mission-oriented, 14; specialized cultures of, 12

Responsibility, moral, 5, 64

Revisionism, historical, 2

*Rhetoric (*Aristotle), 75

Ricardo, David, 156

Risk assessment, 141

Sartre, Jean-Paul, 3, 34*n3*, 48, 168, 169, 170, 171

Saussure, Ferdinand de, 107, 110

Schilpp, Paul, 35*n5*

Science: alienation of history of and philosophy of, 22, 23; autarchic, 69; chance in, 69; disciplinary boundaries in, 34*n2*; as emancipation from theology, 111; experimental *vs.* speculative, 60, 61; governed by necessity, 69; historiography of, 16; legitimation of, 165; linear model of policy of, 14; moral riskiness in, 158; motion in, 142; paradigm boundaries in, 36*n9*; philosophy of, 21, 46; of the plausible, 3, 164; politics and, 11; relation to history, 2; relevance of, 153; self-contained, 69; social status of, 2; valorization of linear models of, 36*n9*

Scientific method, 27

Scientific Revolution, 16, 17, 25; historical significance of, 26

Simulation: deterministic, 89; as representation, 89–90

Simultaneity, 56

Singer, Peter, 34*n1*

Skinner, B.F., 11

Slavery: economic sustainability of, 30, 31

Smith, Adam, 156

Smocovitis, V. Betty, 46, 57, 62, 83, 143, 144, 153, 155, 176, 177, 182, 183, 184

Social: action, 50, 60; class, 14; cohesion, 155; engineering, 141; interaction, 117; justice, 145; order, 12, 14; reality, 177; relations, 41; theory, 79

Socialism, 14

Social science: classical period of, 52; determinism and, 3; interpretivist, 10; narrative in, 52; probability and, 73

Sovereignty, 100

Space, 54, 55; properties of, 20; and time, 121

Spinoza, Baruch, 168

Spontaneity, 81; antimony of, 91; determination and, 77; power and, 77; realm of, 79

Underdeterminism, 10*fig,* 15, 36*n10*; chaos and, 16; in Christianity, 36*n13*; conceptions of history in, 17; decisionmaking in, 18; excesses of, 21; history and, 20; inscrutability of contingency in, 18; interpretations of, 16, 17; irreplaceability of people in, 18; modal logics of history in, 18, 19*fig;* perspective represented by, 25; perspectives of the past/future in, 17; sustainability of slavery and, 30, 31; unified origin in, 17

Universality: confused with necessity, 90; loss of, 111

Universe: alternate branching, 26; common denominator, 53; determination of future history of, 123; disciplinary boundaries and, 34*n2*; geocentric view of, 20; history of, 118; parallel, 26; perceptions of, 55; as self-contained machine, 15; trajectories in, 118, 119

Value(s), 3; challenged by postmodernity, 107; commitments, 31; constructed, 150; expected, 3, 123; logic of, 111; realization of, 31; self-fulfilling prophecies and, 31

Verdi, Giuseppe, 80, 81, 82

Vienna Circle, 12

Voluntarism, 34*n3*

von Kries, J., 77, 78

von Neumann, John, 73, 74, 129

Waddington, Conrad, 35*n7*

Wagner, Richard, 82, 83

Walden Two (Skinner), 11

Wallerstein, Immanuel, 1, 3, 41, 42, 49, 50, 51, 53, 55, 60, 62, 64, 65, 90, 91, 92, 95, 96, 97, 98, 100, 103, 105, 106, 108, 109, 137, 138, 139, 140, 143, 145, 156, 158, 163–165, 172, 174, 177, 179, 180, 182, 183

Weber, Max, 97, 138, 170

Welfare programs, 31

Wiles, Andrew, 44

Will: clash of, 34*n3*; freedom to/of, 7, 8, 9, 23, 79, 95, 96, 167

Williams, Raymond, 145

The Will to Believe (James), 5

Wilson, E.O., 35*n7,* 58

Worldview: evolutionary, 6, 6*fig,* 16, 34*n2*; freedom/determinism binary in, 5–33; mechanical, 6, 6*fig,* 10, 16, 34*n2*